599
ALL   Allen, Missy

             Dangerous mammals

DUE DATE	BRODART	10/94	19.95
MAY 1 1			
NOV 29 99			
NOV 27 2001			

DANGEROUS MAMMALS

The Encyclopedia of Danger

DANGEROUS ENVIRONMENTS

DANGEROUS FLORA

DANGEROUS INSECTS

DANGEROUS MAMMALS

DANGEROUS NATURAL PHENOMENA

DANGEROUS PLANTS AND MUSHROOMS

DANGEROUS PROFESSIONS

DANGEROUS REPTILIAN CREATURES

DANGEROUS SPORTS

DANGEROUS WATER CREATURES

CHELSEA HOUSE PUBLISHERS

The Encyclopedia of Danger

DANGEROUS MAMMALS

Missy Allen
Michel Peissel

CHELSEA HOUSE PUBLISHERS

New York   Philadelphia

On the cover Watercolor painting of a grizzly bear by Michel Peissel.

Chelsea House Publishers

Editor-in-Chief Richard S. Papale
Managing Editor Karyn Gullen Browne
Copy Chief Philip Koslow
Picture Editor Adrian G. Allen
Art Director Maria Epes
Assistant Art Director Howard Brotman
Manufacturing Director Gerald Levine
Systems Manager Lindsey Ottman

Encyclopedia of Danger
Editor Karyn Gullen Browne

Staff for DANGEROUS MAMMALS
Associate Editor Terrance Dolan
Production Editor Marie Claire Cebrián-Ume
Designer Diana Blume
Copy Editor Martin Mooney
Editorial Assistant Karen Hirsch

3 5 7 9 8 6 4 2

Library of Congress Cataloging–in–Publication Data

Peissel, Michel.
Dangerous Mammals/Michel Peissel, Missy Allen.
p. cm.—(The Encyclopedia of danger)
Includes bibliographical references and index.
Summary: Examines 24 dangerous mammals found around the world, from the African elephant to the wolf.
ISBN 0–7910–1790–7
     0–7910–1935–7 (pbk.)
1. Dangerous animals—Juvenile literature. 2. Mammals—Juvenile literature.
[1. Dangerous animals. 2. Mammals.] I. Allen, Missy. II. Title. III. Series: Peissel, Michel, Encyclopedia of danger.
QL100.P44 1992
599—dc20
91–45264
CIP
AC

CONTENTS

THE ENCYCLOPEDIA OF DANGER

"Mother Nature" is not always motherly; often, she behaves more like a wicked aunt than a nurturing parent. She can be unpredictable and mischievous—she can also be downright dangerous.

The word *danger* comes from the Latin *dominium*—"the right of ownership"—and Mother Nature guards her domain jealously indeed, using an ingenious array of weapons to punish trespassers. These weapons have been honed to a fatal perfection during millions of years of evolution, and they can be insidious or overwhelming, subtle or brutal. There are insects that spray toxic chemicals and insects that go on the march in armies a million strong; there are snakes that spit venom and snakes that smother the life from their victims; there are fish that inflict electric shocks and fish that can strip a victim to the bones; there are even trees that exude poisonous gases and flowers that give off a sweet—and murderous—perfume.

Many citizens of the modern, urban, or suburban world have lost touch with Mother Nature. This loss of contact is dangerous in itself; to ignore her is to invite her wrath. Every year, hundreds of children unknowingly provoke her anger by eating poisonous berries or sucking deadly leaves or roots; others foolishly cuddle toxic toads or step on venomous sea creatures. Naive travelers expose themselves to a host of unsuspected natural dangers, but you do not have to fly to a faraway country to encounter one of Mother Nature's sentinels; many of them can be found in your own apartment or backyard.

The various dangers featured in these pages range from the domestic to the exotic. They can be found throughout the world, from the deserts to the polar regions, from lakes and rivers to the depths of the oceans, from subterranean passages to high mountaintops, from rain forests to backyards, from barns to bathrooms. Which of these dangers is the most dangerous? We have prepared a short list of 10 of the most formidable weapons in Mother Nature's arsenal:

Grizzly bear.   Undoubtedly one of the most ferocious creatures on the planet, the grizzly needs little provocation to attack, maul, and maybe even eat a person. (There is something intrinsically more terrifying about an animal that will not only kill you but eat you—and not necessarily in that order—as well.) Incredibly strong, a grizzly can behead a moose with one swipe of its paw. Imagine what it could do to *you*.

Cape buffalo.   Considered by many big-game hunters to be the most evil-tempered animal in all of Africa, Cape buffalo bulls have been known to toss a gored body—perhaps the body of an unsuccessful big-game hunter—around from one pair of horns to another.

Weever fish.   The weever fish can inflict a sting so agonizing that victims stung on the finger have been known to cut off the finger in a desperate attempt to relieve the pain.

Estuarine crocodile.   This vile human-eater kills and devours an estimated 2,000 people annually.

Great white shark.   The infamous great white is a true sea monster. Survivors of great white shark attacks—and survivors are rare—usually face major surgery, for the great white's massive jaws inflict catastrophic wounds.

Army ants.   Called the "Genghis Khans of the insect world" by one entomologist, army ants can pick an elephant clean in a few days and routinely cause the evacuation of entire villages in Africa and South America.

Blue-ringed octopus.   This tentacled sea creature is often guilty of over-kill; it frequently injects into the wound of a single human victim enough venom to kill 10 people.

Introduction

Black widow spider.   The female black widow, prowler of crawl spaces and outhouses, produces a venom that is 15 times as potent as rattlesnake poison.

Lorchel mushroom.   Never make a soup from these mushrooms—simply inhaling the fumes would kill you.

Scorpion.   Beware the sting of this nasty little arachnid, for in Mexico it kills 10 people for every 1 killed by poisonous snakes.

DANGEROUS MAMMALS

According to zoologists, we live in the Age of Mammals, which began about 65 million years ago. Mammals, members of the Mammalia class of animals, are considered to be the most highly developed of all the creatures on Earth. Mammals first appeared 190 million years ago during the Triassic Period, and many species of mammals, such as the dire wolf and the saber–toothed tiger, have since become extinct. Today, there are about 4,000 living species of mammals, and they can be found in almost any environment or geographic location.

There are many biological features that make mammals different from—and in some ways superior to—other kinds of animals, such as fish, reptiles, and insects. One of the most distinctive characteristics is the presence of mammary glands—which produce nutritious milk for infant mammals—in females; this is where the term *mammal* comes from. The most important difference between mammals and other animals, however, is the size of their brain. Mammals have large brains compared to all the other creatures on the planet; therefore, they are recognized as being more intelligent than, and hence superior to, nonmammalians.

Mammals differ widely in appearance, size, habits, and manner of locomotion. Some are ugly; others are beautiful. Some are huge; others are small. Many species are social, whereas others are more independent and lead relatively solitary lives. The snow leopard is graceful and pretty; the platypus is not. The shrew is very small; the elephant is very big. The wolf is highly social and lives in familial packs; the tiger travels alone. Kangaroos hop, dolphins swim, and vampire bats fly.

Dangerous Mammals

Some of the mammals examined on the following pages are dangerous only to certain other animals. Some pose a threat to humans. Which is the most dangerous mammal? Is it the silent, stalking leopard? Is it the raging grizzly? Is it the vicious Cape buffalo? The answer in each case is no, for these creatures live in balance with their environment and with each other. Their behavior, however savage and horrifying, falls within the bounds of a natural order. But the species of mammal that can truly be called the most dangerous exhibits behavior that is criminal rather than natural. It is the only creature to engage in the wanton destruction of its own environment and its own species (not to mention the destruction of other species). How ironic it is that this species of mammal considers itself to be the most intelligent of them all. Perhaps *Homo sapiens* could learn a few lessons from its "inferior" fellow mammals. Or perhaps the Age of Mammals is coming to an end.

KEY

HABITAT

FOREST

SEA

WOOD/TRASH

TOWNS

SHORE

GRASS/FIELDS

MOUNTAINS

SWAMP/MARSH

GARDEN

FRESH WATER

JUNGLE

BUILDING

DESERT

CITIES

11

KEY

HOW IT GETS PEOPLE

INGESTION

TOUCH

STING

BITE

SPIT

SPRAY

MAUL

CLIMATIC ZONE

TEMPERATE

TROPICAL

ARCTIC

MORTALITY

ONE

TWO

THREE

FOUR

DANGEROUS MAMMALS

AFRICAN ELEPHANT

HOW IT GETS PEOPLE

Species: Loxodonta africana

CLIMATIC ZONE

HABITAT

HABITAT

RATING

The African elephant is the true monarch of the animal kingdom. Jumbo, the largest African elephant ever held in captivity, stood 11 feet tall at the shoulder and weighed more than 6 tons. As part of showman P. T. Barnum's traveling circus, Jumbo astonished millions of Americans and Canadians from 1882 to 1885. Perhaps the most astonished of all these people was the man driving the express freight train that crashed into Jumbo in Ontario in 1885. His amazement at seeing the mammoth lumbering toward him on the train tracks did not last long, however, for the head-to-head collision killed him and destroyed his train. The crash also killed Jumbo.

Jumbo was a friendly elephant—he gave rides to an estimated 1 million children during his circus career—and the train wreck he caused was accidental. Imagine the destructive potential of an elephant of that size that was *angry*. In Africa, tales of the wrath of rogue elephants are legion, for these creatures fear nothing and when aroused will attack anything, including people, cars, trucks, and even houses. (Rogue elephants are solitary, elder males that have been driven from the herd by younger, stronger males.) A game warden in Africa tells the story of an elephant that charged a car (the occupants had managed to escape), impaled it on its tusks, and then threw it so far that the vehicle "bounced like a great ball." In his book *Elephants*, Richard Carrington recounts an episode about a man who stopped his car and got out to offer an elephant a bun. The elephant, which apparently did not like buns, seized the man with its trunk, tossed him high in the air, and then kneeled on him, crushing the man to a pulp. Another infamous rogue would seize travelers on a certain road, hold them against the ground with one foot, and then pull their limbs off, one by one.

Name/Description

The African elephant (*Loxodonta africana*) is the largest land animal on earth, standing as tall as 13 feet at the shoulder, measuring as long as 32 feet from the tip of the trunk to the end of the tail, and weighing as much

as 8 tons. The most remarkable feature of the elephant is the trunk; its 40,000 muscles and tendons make it both a powerful and a delicate instrument. At the tip of the trunk are two "fingers" that allow an elephant to pick up something as small as a peanut; it can also use the trunk to haul fallen trees. The African elephant's gigantic fanlike ears can grow as large as 30 square feet and can span 10 feet from ear tip to ear tip. When flapped, the ears act as cooling organs. The elephant's tusks are specialized incisor teeth in the upper jaw; they continue to grow throughout the animal's life. The longest tusks on record measured 11 feet 5 inches and 11 feet, respectively, and had a combined weight of 110 pounds. (The ivory tusks have always been greatly sought after by humans—during the early 20th century about 100,000 elephants were killed yearly for their tusks—and this has led to the tragic near-extinction of this marvelous creature.) Pregnant females have a gestation period of 24 months, and the average life span of an elephant is 70 years.

Elephants are social animals, highly intelligent, protective, and faithful. They frequently come to one another's aid, even attempting to get a wounded or dying friend back on its feet. When an elephant dies, other elephants will "bury" it with earth and leaves and then stand guard over it for a period. A mother elephant was once seen carrying her dead calf on her tusks, refusing to be separated from it. When a herd is threatened, the elephants form a protective circle around their young.

Injury

An angry elephant can inflict catastrophic injuries. For treatment, see Bites, Gorings, Maulings, and Shock, p. 110.

Prevention

- Never get between a baby elephant and its mother or other adult members of the herd.
- Avoid solitary males, or rogues; they are often in a surly mood.

When P. T. Barnum's African elephant, Jumbo, was struck by a train, the force of the impact derailed the locomotive and two cars and killed the engineer and Jumbo.

- Avoid elephants in *musth*, or sexual heat. A sure sign of musth is a flow of dark, oily liquid from a gland situated between the elephant's eye and ear. Elephants in musth are volatile and unpredictable.

BABOON

CLIMATIC ZONE

Genera: Chaeropithecus and Comopithecus

RATING

HOW IT GETS PEOPLE

HOW IT GETS PEOPLE

HABITAT

HABITAT

Baboons are arguably the most dangerous of all the monkeys; they are unquestionably the most hostile. Traveling in marauding bands of up to 300 members, baboons often attack en masse. They have been known to launch raids on farms and villages in Africa and Asia, pillaging homes, stampeding cattle, destroying crops, and even kidnapping human infants, whom, according to legend, they then raise as baboons. Highly intelligent, these warrior monkeys use weapons in battle, throwing stones or rolling boulders down hillsides onto their enemies (which are usually other baboons). When their "army" is at rest, sentries are posted around the perimeter of their encampment. Baboons have excellent

Baboon

eyesight and an excellent sense of smell, as well as acutely developed hearing, and thus it is almost impossible for an enemy to sneak up on them. During the First World War, a baboon named Jackie became a mascot and sentry for the Third South African Infantry Regiment and saw front–line combat against Turkish and German forces. Wounded in action, Jackie was made a corporal and awarded a medal for valor. In 1919, the baboon, seated atop a captured German howitzer, took part in a London victory procession.

Name/Description

Baboons are large, powerful, ground–dwelling monkeys of the genera *Chaeropithecus* and *Comopithecus*. The five species of the *Chaeropithecus* genus are found in Africa. *Comopithecus hamadryus*, also known as the sacred baboon, is found in both Africa and Asia, and is thus the only species of primate (except for *Homo sapiens*) found on two continents.

Baboons have large heads, arms as long as their legs, and they walk or run on all fours. Males are twice the size of females and have thick manes. Baboons look like dogs, facially; they have long doglike muzzles

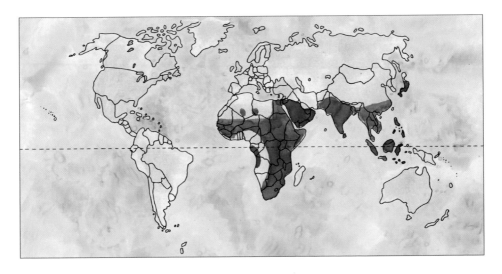

and large canine fangs. Fluted ridges run down each side of the nose, and a fierce brow protrudes over their close-set eyes. Baboons are omnivorous (feeding on both animal and vegetable substances), and their favorite foods are scorpions and prickly pears. They often carry food in large cheek pouches. Preferring rocky terrain, baboons can also be found in the bush. They sleep in trees and on high cliffs and ledges, where they are safe from predators such as cheetahs and leopards.

Life in a baboon troop is both savage and tender. All male baboons jealously guard their mates, and in some species, if a female is "unfaithful" she is punished with death. Female baboons are very protective of their young, as are the other members of the troop, who like to touch, fondle, and play with the babies. For the first four or five months after birth, infant baboons cling tightly to their mother's belly, where they nurse and even sleep. After five or sixth months the baby will start riding on the mother's back, jockeylike, near the tail. At this age the young baboons become adventurous and full of tricks; mother baboons call to wandering offspring by loudly smacking their lips. Mothers spend a lot of time grooming their young, and all members of the troop take turns grooming each other. Not only is grooming important for good hygiene—baboons remove dirt and parasites from one another's coat and clean wounds and scabs—it also has a soothing social influence, reinforcing the troop's cohesion. In case of attack, the females will run away with their young while the males prepare to fight.

Injury

Baboons in the wild are ferocious fighters. The baboon's primary weapons are its powerful jaws and large, sharp teeth. For treatment of bite wounds, see Bites, Gorings, Maulings, and Shock, p. 110.

Prevention

- Baboons are combative and unpredictable. Never venture too close to a troop, and never corner or trap a baboon in a place where it has no

Baboon

Baboons have been known to occasionally attack homes and kidnap human children.

avenue of escape. When cornered, these creatures will attack and fight to the death.

- If you find yourself in a confrontation with baboons, back away from them slowly. Never turn your back; human victims are most frequently bitten on the back of the legs and on the buttocks while fleeing from a baboon.

BLACK RHINOCEROS

HOW IT GETS PEOPLE

Species: Diceros bicornus

CLIMATIC ZONE

HABITAT

HABITAT

RATING

As short-tempered as they are shortsighted, black rhinoceroses have been known to toss people into the air with their horns and to turn over jeeps and even trucks. The black rhino is so myopic that it may not be able to clearly see a person or vehicle only 65 feet away, but a disturbing scent or sound is often enough to send the ornery brute crashing off through the brush like a runaway locomotive; sometimes it will run for miles before it finally tires. Black rhinos will charge just about any-thing—people, vehicles, houses, and even elephants! They have also been known to storm into a campsite at night, disrupting a peaceful dinner around the campfire.

Black Rhinoceros

In his book *Classic African Animals*, professional hunter Tony Dyer recounts his own run-in with an indignant black rhino: "There was a sudden snort, and a rhinoceros horn swept up my right trouser leg. The horn entered my trouser cuff and ripped up to the level of my belt to smash my rifle stock. . . . The horn continued its swift progress and caught me under the right arm, at which time I achieved instant levitation. My short spell airborne ended with a heavy fall on the rhino's back, followed by the ignominy of a quick tumble to the ground." The rhino then seemed to lose interest in Dyer and wandered off. "I undoubtably owe my life," Dyer concluded, "to his magnanimity."

Name/Description

The black rhinoceros (*Diceros bicornus*) of Africa is a large—10 to 12 feet long and 4 to 5 feet high at the shoulder—thick-skinned, plant-eating mammal of the family Rhinocerotidae. Its massive head has two horns; the anterior horn, which can grow up to 50 inches, is much larger than the posterior horn. Sometimes the beginnings of a third horn are visible. Black rhinos are hairless and have a prehensile (adapted for grasping)

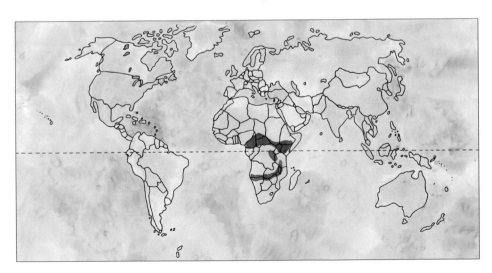

upper lip for eating foliage and berries. They have a good sense of smell and hearing but very poor eyesight. Despite their bulk—they can weigh up to 3,000 pounds—and their stubby legs, rhinos can gallop at speeds of up to 28 miles per hour. They are also excellent swimmers. Mostly nocturnal, they usually inhabit grasslands and forested areas.

Although it was at one time common across the African continent, the black rhino is now endangered, having virtually disappeared in many African countries. The primary reasons for the black rhino's tragic demise are habitat disruption and poachers, who hunt the rhino for its horn, which they then sell. In northern India, powdered rhino horn, which contains the protein keratin, is valued as an aphrodisiac, and in China and other parts of the Far East it is reputed to have various medicinal properties as well. Rhino hooves, blood, and urine are also sold for medicinal use. But the most profitable market for the rhino's horn is the tiny Arab state of Yemen, where men prize the *djambia*. A traditional symbol of manhood, the djambia is a decorative dagger with a handle carved from a rhino horn. Stiff penalties for poaching have been instituted in some African countries—in Zimbabwe, rhino poachers are shot on sight—and many nations have banned trade in rhino horns, but a thriving black market continues to tempt poachers.

Injury

A rhino barreling along at full speed is a juggernaut and is best observed from afar. People who find themselves on the wrong end of a black rhino charge usually sustain serious injury. For treatment, see Bites, Gorings, Maulings, and Shock, p. 110.

Prevention

- When in the proximity of a black rhino, stay upwind and avoid making excess noise or movements.

- In rhino territory, avoid wearing bright-colored clothing.

Black Rhinoceros

The short-tempered black rhinoceros may attack
both people and the cars they ride in.

CAPE BUFFALO

HOW IT GETS PEOPLE

Species: Syncerus caffer

CLIMATIC ZONE

HABITAT

HABITAT

HABITAT

RATING

Ask an experienced big-game hunter what the most dangerous animal in Africa is and he probably will not say "lion" or "elephant" or "rhino" or "cobra." Instead, he will most likely cite the Cape buffalo. A species of wild oxen, the Cape buffalo is big, fast, wily, and so evil tempered that words such as *vindictive*, *vengeful*, and *malevolent* are often used to describe it.

Even the boldest of hunters balk at the idea of pursuing a Cape buffalo into the bush—especially if it is wounded. In this scenario, the hunted becomes the hunter, and vice versa. The enraged buffalo will conceal itself in the shadows and foliage, waiting. When its tormentor draws close, the animal will burst from its cover in an explosive charge. The hunter, at best, will have time to get off one shot. And even if he is an expert marksman carrying a powerful rifle, his chances of dropping the onrushing beast are slim, for a bullet to the body will not even slow the Cape buffalo because of its tough hide, and its brain is largely protected by the thick base of its massive horns, which can easily turn away a bullet. If his aim is anything less than perfect, the hunter will find himself at the mercy of the beast, which means he will be repeatedly trampled and gored until his remains are unrecognizable. If there are other Cape buffaloes about, they may then play "catch" with the corpse, tossing it from one pair of horns to another.

Name/Description

The Cape buffalo (*Syncerus caffer*), also known as the African buffalo, lives in herds of 25 to 400 in sub–Saharan Africa. It is quite large, standing four to five feet at the shoulder and weighing up to three–quarters of a ton.

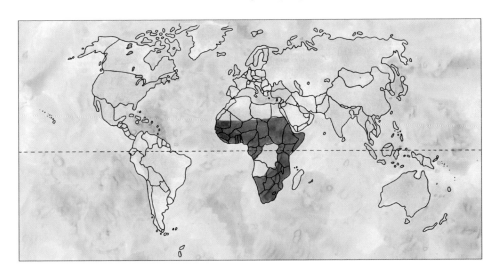

The head, neck, and shoulders are heavily built and support huge crescent horns. The hide of the Cape buffalo is thick, tough, and brownish black in color. The Cape buffalo's broad hooves are adapted to the lowland swamps, marshes, and lagoons it frequents.

The Cape buffalo likes to pass the hot African days by swimming and wallowing. It uses its horns to shovel up mud for plasters, which protect its skin from irritating gadflies. Sometimes the Cape buffalo will immerse itself in water and stay there, with just its nose above the surface, for long periods of time. A grazer, the Cape buffalo lives on grass but will also nibble on leaves and twigs when grass is sparse. Breeding occurs year–round, and the gestation period is about a year. The only creature that the Cape buffalo seems to fear is the lion. The Cape buffalo population is on the decline because of disease and uncontrolled hunting.

Injury

Anyone who survives an encounter with an angry Cape buffalo is lucky. For treatment, see Bites, Gorings, Maulings, and Shock, p. 110.

Prevention

• Unless it is directly threatened or attacked, the Cape buffalo usually minds its own business. Herds should be given a wide berth in case of stampede. If a Cape buffalo comes after you, find a tree and climb it—with extreme haste.

After an attack, Cape buffaloes have been known to toss a victim's body from horn to horn as if it were a ball.

When disturbed, the usually passive Cape buffalo may relentlessly gore and trample its victims.

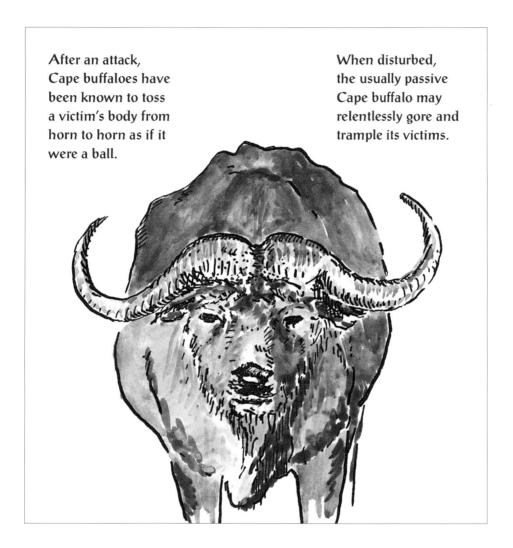

COUGAR

HOW IT GETS PEOPLE

Species: Felis concolor

HOW IT GETS PEOPLE

HABITAT

HABITAT

HABITAT

CLIMATIC ZONE

CLIMATIC ZONE

RATING

For centuries, ranchers from British Columbia to Argentina have regarded the cougar as a marauding outlaw and thus fair game to be shot by any hunter who managed to track one down. The cougar has done little to improve its reputation. A prodigious and wanton butcher of livestock, this big cat has reportedly slaughtered 50 sheep in a single night. The cougar will attack lambs, sheep, cows, and even full-grown horses. And it will, on occasion, attack a human.

Cougar

Along the Campbell River in British Columbia, a cougar, intent on killing a 63-year-old man he had been stalking, hurled itself through a window to get at the man inside his house. A hunting partner of former president Theodore Roosevelt was mauled savagely by a cougar that leapt down upon him from a high, rocky ledge. Roosevelt, a wildlife enthusiast and an avid big-game hunter, described cougars as "ferocious and bloodthirsty," and his unfortunate friend no doubt agreed.

Name/Description

The cougar (*Felis concolor*), also known as the mountain lion, the panther, or the puma, formerly roamed the Americas from Alaska to Cape Horn and thus had the widest distribution of any mammal on the two continents, aside from *Homo sapiens*. The largest species of felid in North America—males can grow to six feet in length and can weigh as much as 230 pounds—the cougar has shown the ability to adapt to any environment in the wild, from tropical southern rain forests to rocky, mountainous regions of the North and West, although hunting, depletion of its food sources, and the expansion of the human population has drastically narrowed the cougar's viable natural habitats.

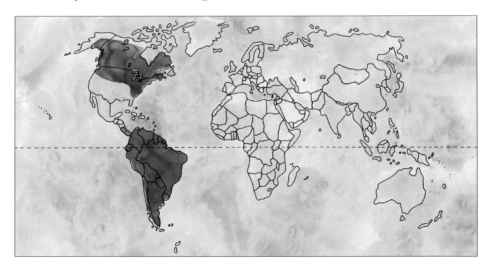

Dangerous Mammals

Leonine in color, the cougar is superbly athletic, with a small head; small, roundish ears; a long neck; short, powerful jaws; an elongated body; and powerful hindquarters that allow it to make truly astonishing leaps. (One cougar was seen to make a 39-foot bound.) It is a swift runner, an excellent swimmer, and can move with a blinding quickness and a startling agility.

Primarily nocturnal, cougars hunt with a skill and daring to match that of any of the world's big cats. Although its sense of smell is relatively poor, it has remarkable eyesight. Its favorite hunting method is to lie in ambush on a high ledge or tree branch and then to leap down upon its unsuspecting victim. Deer is the cougar's favorite food, although it will also eat other hoofed animals, beavers, porcupines (ouch!), and hares. After a successful hunt, the cougar will usually drag the kill to a secluded place to feed. Any leftovers are carefully concealed and then eaten at the cat's leisure during the following days. Loners, cougars take pains to avoid one another, except during their brief mating period. About once every two years females will produce a litter of up to six offspring, which remain with their mother for up to a year before striking out on their own.

Injury

The cougar's teeth and claws can inflict serious damage on a victim. For treatment, see Bites, Gorings, Maulings, and Shock, p. 110.

Infection

Not only are their attacks ferocious; cougars are also carriers of rabies. Two boys were attacked by a female cougar near Morgan Hill, California, during the early 1960s. They were badly mauled and bitten, as was a young woman who attempted to help them. Although they survived the actual attack, one of the boys and the young woman died of rabies shortly thereafter. For the symptoms and treatment of that disease, see Rabies, p. 113.

Cougar

**The most powerful jumper in North America,
cougars have been known to leap through windows
to reach their prey.**

Prevention

• Cougars are notoriously elusive, especially when humans are around, and your chances of seeing one, never mind being attacked by one, are slim. Nevertheless, if you are in cougar territory, and especially if you are riding a horse—cougars have a penchant for attacking mounted humans—it would be prudent to keep your eyes open when you are passing through hilly, rocky country. Remember, cougars like to attack from above.

DUCKBILL PLATYPUS

HOW IT GETS PEOPLE

Species: Ornithorhynchus anatinus

HABITAT

CLIMATIC ZONE

CLIMATIC ZONE

RATING

When stuffed specimens of the duckbill platypus were first brought back from Australia to Europe in the 18th century, scientists dismissed them as a hoax. Surely, thought the scientists, this bizarre creature, which looked like a cross between a beaver and a duck, could only be the work of a deeply disturbed taxidermist. But young G. H. Sargent of Currumben, Australia, could have testified that the platypus was no hoax. At the age of 12, Sargent caught a platypus in Australia's North Pine River and took the strange creature home with him. That evening, as Sargent was showing his new pet to some interested performers from a traveling circus, the animal became alarmed—perhaps at the thought of spending the rest of its days as a freak in a sideshow—and struck Sargent in the wrist and stomach with the horny spurs on its hind legs. "The pain was very severe," said Sargent, "like a nerve pain, and left me feeling shocked and sick for some minutes. The hand immediately began to swell and was soon so puffy that no knuckles were visible. The whole arm became very hot and a lump developed in the arm pit." As soon as he had recovered, Sargent returned the prickly platypus to the river.

Name/Description

The duckbill platypus (*Ornithorhynchus anatinus*), a single genus, single species member of the Monotremata order, is one of only two venomous mammals on earth. (The other is the shrew.) It is also one of the strangest-looking creatures on the planet; scientists originally called it Paradoxicus—the paradox—because of its incongruous behavior and anatomy. The platypus growls like a dog, swims like a duck, digs like a mole, and stings like a bee. About the size of a beaver, it has dense, water-repellent fur, a flat tail like a beaver's, a fleshy bill much like a duck's, and webbed feet with clawed toes. Instead of teeth, the platypus has hard, ridged plates for crushing and chewing food.

The platypus is aquatic, frequenting freshwater streams and rivers. It hunts for food underwater during the early morning and evening,

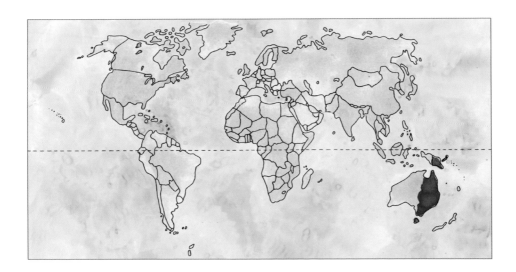

feeding mostly on crayfish, shrimps, water insects, snails, tadpoles, worms, and small fish. When it is submerged, the eyes and ears of the platypus are covered by skin folds, and thus it hunts by sense of touch alone; its sensitive bill has been developed for this task. When it catches food underwater, the platypus stores it in cheek pouches and eats it once it is back on dry ground. A big eater, it can consume half its own weight in food in a single day. Platypuses live in underground burrows with underwater entrances. The female platypus lays its eggs and raises its young in a separate burrow.

On the ankles of the hind legs of the male platypus are hollow, inward-pointing spurs that are connected to poison glands. When threatened, the spurs become erect and the platypus injects venom into its enemy with a convulsive kicking motion, usually stinging with both spurs. The spurs are defensive weapons, developed for territorial and mating disputes among males.

Toxicology

Platypus venom has been identified as a solution of largely albuminous proteins, with some proteinase present as well.

Symptoms

Symptoms of platypus envenomization begin with an immediate and often intense pain, followed by swelling, numbness in the area of the wound, dizziness, restlessness, weakness, and possibly some glandular swelling.

Treatment

Hot baths for the affected part of the body have proven effective. Recovery is usually uneventful and takes only a few days.

Prevention

Do not disturb.

Duckbill Platypus

When threatened, the duckbill platypus injects its victims with a painful, long-lasting poison.

FERRET

HOW IT GETS PEOPLE

Species: Mustela putorius furo

CLIMATIC ZONE

HABITAT

HABITAT

RATING

During the 1980s in the United States, ferrets, small, slinky, weasel–like mammals with luxuriant fur, became common household pets. They were especially popular among dormitory–dwelling college students and urban apartment dwellers who wanted a pet but did not have enough room for a dog (and who apparently did not like cats). In 1988, 50,000 ferrets were sold in the United States. But before the decade was out, these ferrets, once described as "ideal yuppie biochattel," began to display a penchant for ripping the flesh from the faces of sleeping human babies. The ferret fad has since died down, and in many places private ownership is now illegal.

Ferret

Ferrets have had a long and occasionally productive relationship with *Homo sapiens*. The Egyptians bred rabbit–hunting ferrets early in the 4th century B.C., and the ancient Chinese bred tame ferrets as pets and vermin exterminators. Hunting rabbits with the help of ferrets was at one time a popular sport in England, Scotland, and other European countries. The ferrets were dispatched into rabbit warrens to chase the rabbits out into the open, where the hunters were waiting to kill them. After the hunt, each hunter would recall his particular ferret by ringing a small bell or making a certain sound that the ferret recognized. England's Queen Victoria was quite fond of ferrets, and especially albino ferrets, although she probably would not have liked them so much if they had attacked the face of little Prince Edward (later King Edward VIII).

Ferrets brought overseas from Europe first became popular in the United States around 1875, when the "ferret man" would wander about rural areas carrying a box of ferrets. For a fee, the ferret man would release his ferrets in barns, basements, and outbuildings. When the ferrets had finished "ferreting out" all the mice and rats, the ferret man

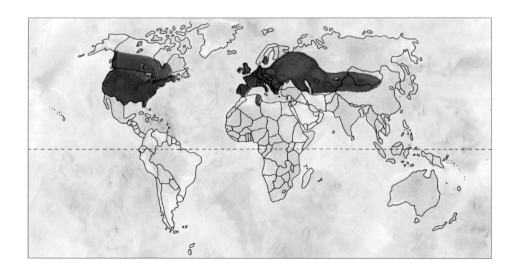

would ring a bell, and his ferrets would come slinking back to him. This rather creepy event succeeded in giving the ferret man a somewhat menacing air, and his customers (not to mention the local mice and rats) were always relieved to see him continue on his way.

Name/Description

The ferret (*Mustela putorius furo*) belongs to the Mustelidae family of mammals and is a cousin of the skunk, otter, mink, and badger. Male ferrets can grow up to two feet in length and weigh as much as eight pounds. Female ferrets are smaller, and newborn ferrets are only two or three inches long. Babies are born with a thin fuzz that eventually thickens into a fine coat; mature ferret coats can be white, silver, sable, cinnamon, or chocolate in color, and they are extremely silky in texture. Some ferrets have masklike facial markings.

The ferret's streamlined, slender body allows it to slide easily into holes and burrows. Prairie dogs are the staple food of ferrets in the wild, although they will also eat rodents, rabbits, amphibians, reptiles, birds and poultry, and fish. Ferrets have scent glands that give off a musky odor, males being more odoriferous than females. Ferrets have a rough-and-tumble courtship ritual in which the male throws his mate about, pushing her to the ground and shaking her. Instead of fighting back, the female will become relaxed and submissive, and mating may last for hours.

Injury

Human victims of ferret attacks are usually small children and babies living in households with pet ferrets. Some behaviorists theorize that the sounds and smells of human infants are particularly attractive to ferrets, which, in the wild, prefer to prey on suckling young. Human victims are usually bitten on the face, and the wounds can be disfiguring. For treatment, see Bites, Gorings, Maulings, and Shock, p. 110.

Ferret

After a rash of maulings, many states have outlawed ferrets as pets, despite their popular appeal.

Infection

Ferrets carry and transmit rabies. The incubation period for rabies in ferrets has not been established, nor is there a licensed rabies vaccine for them—as there is for dogs and cats—and thus there is a serious risk of infection. For symptoms and treatment, see Rabies, p. 113.

Prevention

• Stick with dogs and cats as pets.

GORILLA

HOW IT GETS PEOPLE

Genus: Gorilla

HOW IT GETS PEOPLE

HABITAT

CLIMATIC ZONE

RATING

Truly he reminded me of nothing but some hellish dream creature, a being of that hideous order, half–man, half–beast." Thus did the trader Paul de Chaillu describe the terrifying creature he encountered in the jungles of Africa in the mid–19th century. Unnerved by the "hellish" beast, Chaillu shot and killed it. Early in the 20th century, naturalist Carl Akeley encountered these same animals in the Belgian Congo and found them to be "perfectly amiable and decent creature[s]." Akeley was so taken with the gorillas that he helped found the Albert National Park as a reserve for the endangered ape, and his gorilla exhibit is still on display in New York's American Museum of Natural History.

Gorilla

What is the true nature of the gorilla? Is it King Kong or is it Koko? Many misinformed people still perceive the gorilla as a King Kong, that monstrous, destructive Hollywood ape. Like any creature, gorillas can be dangerous—but only when threatened. Almost all the known victims of gorilla attacks have been poachers who were ruthless enough to hunt and kill gorillas, and it can truly be said that in these cases the gorillas were acting in self-defense. But anyone who has read the works of naturalist Dian Fossey or seen the movie *Gorillas in the Mist* knows that gorillas in general are more akin to Koko, the gentle, playful, and highly intelligent gorilla that has been the subject of a recent study by scientists concerning gorillas' ability to communicate.

Name/Description

The gorilla is the largest of the primates, the mammal order that includes monkeys and humans. Found in the rain forests of equatorial Africa, gorillas weigh only 4 pounds at birth, but a full-grown male can weigh as much as 500 pounds and stand more than 6 feet tall. Females are

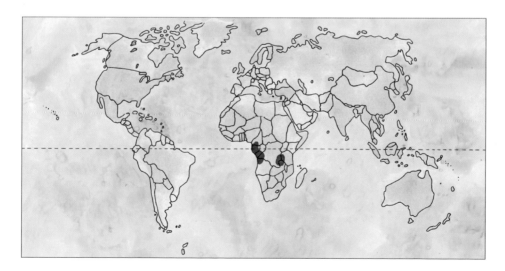

usually half the size of males. Gorillas are highly social; groups of up to 30 gorillas, led by a large, mature male—known as a silverback—travel together to forage. (Gorillas are vegetarians.) At night they build nests; although they are primarily terrestrial apes, being too large for tree climbing, young gorillas and females with infants build their sleeping nests in the lower branches of trees, whereas the males sleep on the ground beneath these trees. Gorillas may sleep for up to 13 hours a day, including a 2- to 3-hour siesta.

Like other great apes, such as the chimpanzee and the orangutan, the gorilla has no tail and walks on all fours, although it can walk upright for short distances. Mothers carry their babies against their bellies for the first four months following birth. The babies will then ride piggyback until they are about two years old. Gorillas are extremely protective of their young. Poachers, in order to capture one young gorilla, have often had to kill all the adults in the family.

Like all the primates, gorillas are extremely intelligent. They can recognize themselves in photographs and mirrors, and they can even make tools; for example, gorillas have been known to fashion large tropical leaves into umbrellas during rainstorms. The aforementioned Koko, using sign language, scored well on a childrens' IQ test.

Injury

The gorilla is timid and mild mannered, having no natural enemies in the wild—except for poachers. (Gorillas have been savagely poached for decades, and they are now on the brink of extinction.) When threatened, a silverback will defend itself and its family with ferocity. A full-grown male gorilla is one of the most powerful creatures on the planet and is easily capable of dismembering a human adversary, although it will more often use its teeth and claws to maul an attacker or intruder. For treatment of wounds, see Bites, Gorings, Maulings, and Shock, p. 110.

Gorilla

**Gorillas can decapitate human beings
with their bare hands.**

Prevention

- A silverback gorilla will respond to a perceived threat by rising up to its full height, pounding its chest with its palms, hooting, roaring, and thrashing about violently. This terrifying display is meant to scare off the intruder, and it usually succeeds. If you find yourself in this unlikely situation, do not run, for then the gorilla will attack. Instead, hold your ground and then back away slowly.

GRIZZLY BEAR

Subspecies: Ursus horribilis

HABITAT

HABITAT

CLIMATIC ZONE

CLIMATIC ZONE

RATING

In researching *Dangerous Mammals*, the authors could find no records of maulings that equaled in ferocity those committed by the grizzly bear. Not even the lion or the tiger inflict such grievous damage on their victims. Consider the testimony of Dr. Barrie Gilbert—given from his hospital bed—who was savagely mauled by a grizzly in Yellowstone National Park in 1977: "The bear started biting me on the back of the head, which felt like a pick-axe scraping along my skull bones. In defense I turned over to kick and push the bear off, but the grizzly bit my face. I recall a deep bite which crushed the bones under my left eye—which was also lost." A grisly tale indeed.

Dr. Gilbert lost an eye and a substantial amount of tissue to his attacker, but Barbara Chapman was not so lucky. On July 27, 1976, Barbara and a friend were hiking in Glacier National Park, Canada, in an area frequented by grizzlies. An experienced naturalist, Barbara had deliberately been making a lot of noise during the hike, in order to avoid startling any bears that might be in the area. Despite their precautions, the two hikers were attacked by a grizzly. Barbara was killed and eaten, and her companion was critically mauled.

The members of the Lewis and Clark expedition had many close brushes with grizzlies. Sent westward by U.S. president Thomas Jefferson in 1804 to follow the Missouri River to its source, they first encountered grizzlies in Montana and were soon involved in several harrowing episodes with the monsters. "I must confess that I do not like the [grizzly]," Captain Meriwether Lewis wrote, "and [I would] rather fight two Indians than one bear." The Indians had great respect for the grizzly

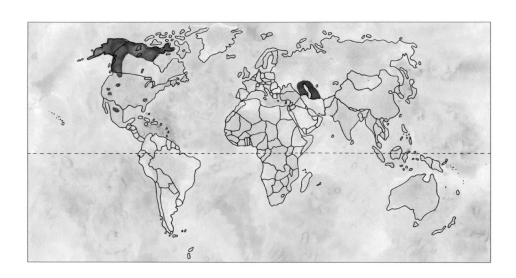

as well. According to a Shasta Indian tale, the god Manitou created the grizzly and made it more powerful and clever then any other creature. But the grizzly proved to be so mighty that Manitou himself had to flee to the top of Mount Shasta to escape it. The Blackfoot Indians believed grizzlies possessed great supernatural and physical powers. Captain Lewis noted that when Indians were about to embark on a grizzly bear hunt, they prepared for it as if they were "about to make war upon a neighboring nation."

Name/Description

The grizzly bear (*Ursus horribilis*) is an irascible subspecies of the giant North American brown bear. The characteristic features of the grizzly bear are a large shoulder hump, a concave face—grizzlies are also known as "dish-faced" bears—and a grayish or silver frosting on its thick, brownish coat of fur. Grizzlies are massive, powerful creatures. They can weigh up to 1,600 pounds and measure 9 feet tall when standing upright. True omnivores, grizzlies will eat almost anything, and in great quantities. An adult grizzly can consume 90 pounds of salmon in a day. At one time, grizzly bears were widely distributed across the North American continent, ranging freely from Mexico to Alaska, but today they survive only in isolated parts of the American West and Canada.

Injury

Grizzlies can literally destroy their victims. For treatment of wounds, see Bites, Gorings, Maulings, and Shock, p. 110.

Prevention

- When hiking in grizzly territory, do not walk too close to salmon streams or berry patches.

- Make a lot of noise in order to warn bears of your approach.

- Grizzlies have a keen sense of smell; if you are observing them, try to stay downwind.

**With a single, powerful blow, a grizzly bear
killed a black bear and hurled it into a tree
five yards away.**

- Keep campsites free of food refuse.

- If you encounter a grizzly, back off slowly, find a tree, and climb it.

- If you are actually attacked by a grizzly, your only chance for survival may be to play dead and hope the bear loses interest. Of course, this is easier said than done. Dr. Ian Stirling, a research biologist with the Canadian Wildlife Service, employed this strategy when he was attacked by a grizzly in British Columbia. "I can still remember rather clearly how annoyed I was with my heart," Stirling recalled. "Here I was, trying to lie still and be quiet while my heart seemed to be thumping like the pistons of a locomotive. It felt as if it was bouncing me off the ground and it seemed the bear could surely hear it." Fortunately for Dr. Stirling, his "tell–tale heart" did not give him away.

HYENA

HOW IT GETS PEOPLE

Species: Crocuta crocuta

HOW IT GETS PEOPLE

HABITAT

HABITAT

HABITAT

HABITAT

HABITAT

CLIMATIC ZONE

CLIMATIC ZONE

RATING

He heard the hyena make a noise just outside the range of the dying fire," Ernest Hemingway wrote in his famous short story "The Snows of Kilimanjaro." In that story, the laughing hyena represents death itself, and indeed, no sound more sinister than the "laugh" of the spotted hyena has ever haunted the African night. Beginning on a low, mournful note, it rises to a high-pitched, demonic cackle that drifts across the savanna. Of all the carnivores of Africa, the spotted hyena has perhaps the ugliest reputation (and probably the ugliest appearance as well). To the native inhabitants, this doglike lurker in the darkness is known as a scavenger, a grave robber, a kidnapper, and a devourer of children. Terry Anderson, the son of a Baptist minister in Kroonstad, South Africa, was dragged from his father's tent in Kruger National Park by a large hyena and carried 30 yards into the bush before his terrified screams brought help. Countless other African children have not been so fortunate, and the hyena's habit of biting a human victim's face has left many survivors of hyena attacks permanently disfigured.

According to legend, hyenas not only laugh but can imitate a man's voice and call him by name, luring him away from the safety of his campfire to be shredded by a hyena pack waiting in the darkness. And indeed, Africans often attempt to appease the hyena as if it were an evil spirit of the night. In Harer, Ethiopia—a place where food of any sort is hard to come by—Africans will nevertheless leave offerings of food at the outskirts of their villages, hoping to satisfy the hyenas' hunger and thus prevent them from entering the village in search of food. In other parts of Africa, inhabitants will put out their dead at sunset; if the corpses are gone by morning, they know that the hyenas have been there.

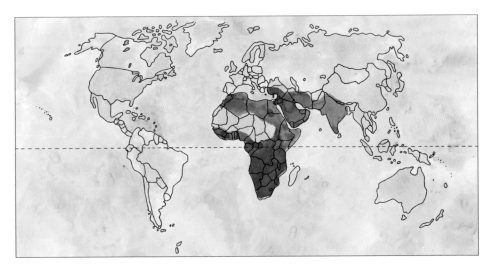

Dangerous Mammals

Name/Description

The spotted hyena (*Crocuta crocuta*), also known as the laughing hyena, is the largest of the two species of hyena found in Africa. (A third species is native to India.) Hideous in appearance, the spotted hyena has an ungainly body—its shoulders are markedly higher than its hindquarters—and a massive head equipped with jaws that are more powerful than the jaws of any other land mammal. The spotted hyena has large ears that seem too large for its body, a bushy tail, a bristling mane like a hog's, and catlike feet with only four toes. Males may grow to be 6 feet long and 3 feet tall at the shoulder and may weigh up to 180 pounds. Spotted hyenas can run up to 40 miles per hour. Usually nocturnal, spotted hyenas spend their days in holes in the ground, in lairs, or in caves. They have a life span of up to 25 years.

Hyenas have long had a reputation for being cowardly scavengers that would rather steal another animal's hard-earned kill than go to the trouble of hunting and killing their own food. This is not altogether true, however. Although hyenas are primarily carrion scavengers, they also hunt for themselves to supplement their diet. The spotted hyena is an efficient and deadly hunter that will usually prey on young or weak herd animals and then devour all of its kill, including the bones. Mealtime among a group of hyenas is a savage, snarling brawl during which a full-grown wildebeest may be torn to pieces and completely eaten within 15 minutes.

Injury

The spotted hyena's jaws are powerful enough to crush human bones, and their sharp canine teeth can inflict deep, ragged wounds. For treatment, see Bites, Gorings, Maulings, and Shock, p. 110.

Prevention

• In hyena country, stay near your campfire at night.

Hyena

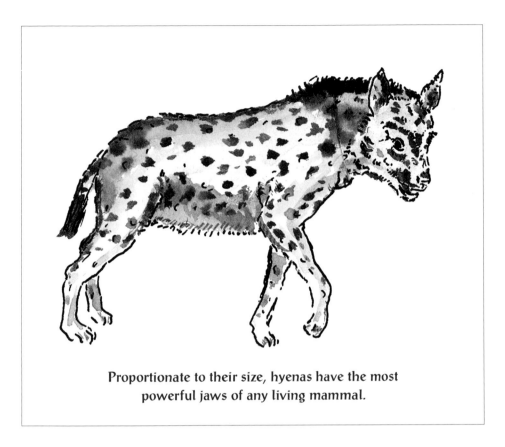

Proportionate to their size, hyenas have the most powerful jaws of any living mammal.

• Hyena species other than the spotted hyena will not attack you during a confrontation if you stand your ground. The spotted hyena, however, is not so easily intimidated, and direct confrontations should be avoided.

JAGUAR

HOW IT GETS PEOPLE

Species: Felis onca

RATING

HABITAT

HABITAT

HABITAT

CLIMATIC ZONE

CLIMATIC ZONE

The jaguar's name is a testament to its prowess as a hunter; *jaguar* comes from the native South American word *jaguara*—"the carnivore that overcomes its prey in a single bound." Patient, powerful, and stealthy, the jaguar's hunting skills are surpassed only by its cousin the leopard, which the jaguar closely resembles. The largest of the New World felids, the jaguar is the true king of the dense South American jungles. Anything that lives in or enters the jaguar's domain is fair game and may become the big cat's dinner. The fecund rain forests provide the jaguar with an extensive menu; deer, domestic cattle, dogs, peccaries, tapirs, sloths, birds, monkeys, foxes, rodents, and turtles and their eggs are all preyed upon by the jaguar. The fearsome alligator presents more of a challenge, but the jaguar will fight and kill the giant reptile, even if it has to go into the water to do so. If it is in a lazy mood, the jaguar may fish for a meal. Stretched out on a low branch overhanging the water, the cat will use its tail as a lure and then flick fish out of the water with its paw.

Sometimes, the jaguar will prey on humans. Travelers in the South American rain forests occasionally report the unnerving experience of having a jaguar stalk them for hours through the jungle. In these cases, the travelers need not have worried overmuch, for the jaguar's visibility was a signal that it had no intention of attacking but was rather escorting them through its territory. If the jaguar had actually been hunting them, they never would have been aware of the cat's presence; most likely, one of the travelers would have simply disappeared from their camp at night while the others slept on undisturbed.

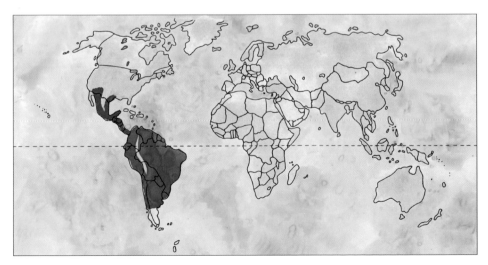

Dangerous Mammals

Name/Description

The jaguar (*Felis onca*) is as beautiful as it is dangerous. Its fur has a base color of golden yellow marked with black rosettes of varying sizes. (Some jaguars are all black or albino, however.) Quite large, males can grow to 9 feet in length and weigh up to 300 pounds. Jaguars have a deep chest, and massive, powerful limbs. Solitary nocturnal predators, they are expert climbers, and when one of the great rivers such as the Amazon or the Orinoco floods the jungle, jaguars live in the trees, moving from one to another with great agility. They are also good swimmers. According to the naturalist Charles Darwin, jaguars were known to seize people off the decks of ships in mid-river during the night. Occasionally, jaguars will emit an earsplitting roar that will fill the jungle, causing flocks of birds to take wing and entire troops of monkeys to chatter and leap about in near panic.

Injury

See Bites, Gorings, Maulings, and Shock, p. 110.

Jaguar

Jaguars lay claim to all the wildlife and livestock that wander through their territory.
They also have been known to knock riders
from their saddles and steal sleeping
children out of hammocks.

KILLER WHALE

HOW IT GETS PEOPLE

Species: Orcinus orca

HABITAT

CLIMATIC ZONE

CLIMATIC ZONE

CLIMATIC ZONE

RATING

Is the killer whale really a killer? Although most marine biologists insist that killer whales present no danger to humans, rumors and stories of attacks on humans persist. The March 28, 1952, edition of the San Francisco *Call-Bulletin* carried the story of two elderly fishermen who were attacked by a "killer whale" near a tiny island off the Sonoma County coast. "We were just about 75 feet from the island when we saw him circling us," reported H. W. Van Buren, one of the fishermen. "There were a lot of seals in the water, but he wasn't going for them. He seemed to be eyeing us. We started rowing as fast as we could to get away. But we didn't get more than 50 feet. He came close and went underneath, bumping the boat. Then he turned and charged right at us, and hit us as hard as he could. He sank his teeth into the boat . . . chewing and twisting . . . trying to break the boat."

The two fishermen survived their close encounter with the sea monster, driving it away—"I took an oar and I just jabbed him right in the eye"—and making it to a nearby island before their damaged boat sank. Surely this incident was concrete proof that killer whales will attack humans. But investigators have since concluded that the two terrified fishermen misidentified their attacker, mistaking a great white shark for a killer whale. In truth, there are no documented cases of killer whale attacks on humans. *Orca*, marine biologists have concluded, presents no significant threat to *Homo sapiens*.

But for seals, penguins, and other warm-blooded mammals that frequent the oceans, the killer whale is a scourge, a marine predator unequaled in speed, power, and cunning.

Dangerous Mammals

Name/Description

The killer whale (*Orcinus orca*), found in ocean waters around the world, is the largest, fastest, most powerful member of the dolphin family. Males grow to an average length of 27 feet and can weigh as much as 6 tons; females are smaller. Both sexes have a streamlined, shiny black body with white undersides, white saddle-shaped markings behind the prominent dorsal fin, and a white spot behind the eyes. The tall, pointed dorsal fin can be as much as six feet high. The male's dorsal fin is straight and leans slightly forward; the female's is curved and looks more like a shark's dorsal.

The eyes are positioned well back on either side of the head, and thus the killer whale cannot see straight ahead.

Killer whales are voracious predators, feeding primarily on warm-blooded mammals, such as seals, whales, porpoises, sea lions, and penguins. Their favorite food is the tongue of a whale. Their powerful jaws—which are capable of cutting a large porpoise in half in a single bite—are equipped with 48 thick, heavy teeth used to tear chunks of meat out of their prey. Like wolves, killer whales hunt in packs, and like wolves, they work as a highly coordinated team, often attacking whales many times their own size. *Orca* travels in packs, or pods, of up to 50 whales. Highly intelligent and vocal like most dolphins, killer whales communicate through various clicking and high-pitched whistling sounds. One of their favorite hunting tactics in Arctic waters is to break up large ice floes by smashing into them from below, thus dumping seals or penguins into the water where they can be easily gobbled up. The killer whale is a ravenous eater and can ingest prodigious amounts of food.

The killer whale can
snap a porpoise in half
with a single bite.

Killer whales have
been nicknamed the
"wolves of the sea."

LEOPARD

HOW IT GETS PEOPLE

Species: Felis pardus

HOW IT GETS PEOPLE

HABITAT

HABITAT

CLIMATIC ZONE

CLIMATIC ZONE

RATING

Big-game hunters regard leopards with awe, for most of them believe that the leopard itself is the greatest hunter of all. Often described as "the perfect killing machine," the leopard is pound for pound the strongest and most athletic of the world's big cats, although it is actually smaller in size than the lion, tiger, and jaguar. It is an excellent runner, swimmer, climber, and leaper; a cunning and preternaturally stealthy hunter; and an efficient and ruthless assassin. When it takes to eating people, it will attack boldly and frequently—sometimes seizing victims from houses in broad daylight—and will not stop its marauding until it has been killed.

The leopard is by far the most prolific of the man-eaters, and in India especially, it has been a scourge. "Leopard Menace In Bhagalpur," read the May 24, 1962, headline of the *Madras Mail*. "The district authorities of Bhagalpur have launched an all-out drive to rid Banka sub-division of the menace of man-eating leopards which, according to local estimates, have claimed about 350 human lives in the last three years. . . . Provision has been made to use tear gas and also to dynamite caves, which were suspected to be the lairs of the man-eaters. A Deputy Magistrate was camping in the jungles of Banka, supervising the drive."

Name/Description

The leopard (*Felis pardus*) is the most adaptable of the big cats, and thus it has the widest geographic distribution. Leopards are populous in sub-Saharan Africa, northern Iran, Israel, the Caucasus Mountains, the

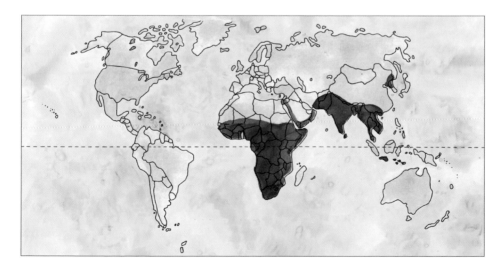

Himalayas (home of the elusive snow leopard, perhaps the most beauti-ful of the big cats), Korea, China, Indochina, Malaysia, and India. A leopard can make itself comfortable in almost any environment, from arid savannas to cold mountain ranges to rain forests, and they have even been known to thrive in suburban areas.

Of all the big cats, leopards most resemble a large version of the common house cat. Powerful, independent, and elegant, the leopard's body can grow to a lithe 7 or 8 feet in length, and it can weigh as much as 180 pounds. The leopard has short legs and a long, thin tail, and its spotted coat resembles the jaguar's. (Stunning, emerald-eyed black leopards are fairly common in some regions.) Its prey includes herd ani-mals, such as antelopes, baboons and monkeys, birds, rodents, snakes, fish, domestic livestock, and dogs (a favorite delicacy).

The leopard has been superbly equipped by nature to hunt and kill. It is a truly astonishing leaper, as monkeys—and people—who have taken refuge in trees and atop houses have learned (often a final lesson), and has been seen easily climbing a tree while carrying in its jaws the carcass of an animal twice its own size. The leopard is an unparalleled stalker; its feet are heavily padded, and its sinuous, gliding gait allows it to move in complete silence. It can freeze in a certain position and remain absolutely motionless for long periods; it uses camouflage and shadows so expertly that it can become virtually invisible; and it often resorts to trickery to catch its prey. In many cultures, the leopard is believed to have supernatural powers and is said to be able to make itself disappear, to turn into a man, and to hypnotize its prey with its eyes. When it strikes, it moves with an explosive quickness.

Injury

Survivors of leopard attacks are rare. If a victim survives the attack itself, he or she often succumbs to trauma or blood poisoning soon after. For symptoms and treatment, see Bites, Gorings, Maulings, and Shock, p. 110.

Leopard

The most athletic member of the feline family, leopards have been deemed "the perfect killing machine."

When hunting, the leopard may roll in the excrement of other mammals in order to disguise its own smell.

LION

HOW IT GETS PEOPLE

Species: Felis leo

HABITAT

CLIMATIC ZONE

RATING

In the year 1898, the worst job in Africa—and perhaps in the world—was to work as a laborer on the construction of a bridge being built over the Tsavo River in southeastern Kenya. The bridge was to be part of a new railroad line that would run between Uganda and the Indian Ocean. The men who worked on the bridge—mostly native Africans and so-called coolies from India—began to disappear from the construction site during the night. At first it was thought that these men were simply leaving on their own, but the disappearances continued. One night, tortured screams woke up the entire camp. The screams were loud at first, just outside the camp, but they quickly grew fainter and fainter, and by the time they had ceased altogether, it was clear that the unfortunate coolie—and the others before him—had been seized and carried off by a man-eating lion.

Fear gripped the workers' camps on the banks of the Tsavo. Construction on the bridge continued nevertheless, and armed guards were posted. But at night, the men continued to vanish. Sometimes two men would be taken in a single night, and it became apparent that two lions were involved in the raids. Often the victims would disappear noiselessly, and their absence would not be noted until morning, when their tents were found empty. At other times, the workers would huddle weeping around their fires at night, listening fearfully to the shrieks of one of their friends as the lions ate him alive. In the morning, search parties would find the remains of the victims; usually only the head was left uneaten. There was no safe place, nowhere to hide, and the lions were seemingly unstoppable. By the time the two man-eaters had been hunted down and killed, they had claimed 28 Indian victims and an untold number of Africans.

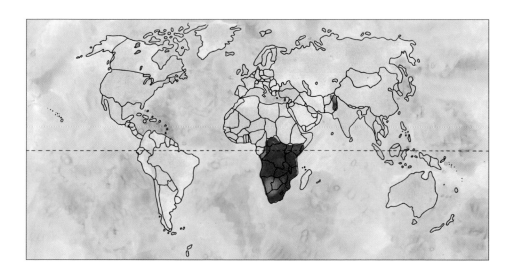

Dangerous Mammals

Name/Description

The lion (*Felis leo*) is a huge, powerful felid found in Africa and south-western Asia. It is, in every aspect, a prodigious animal. A lion is usually about 6 feet long, but some have been known to grow as long as 10 feet and to weigh 500 pounds or more. (Newborn cubs weigh only one pound.) Tawny yellow to reddish brown in color, lions have a broad, massive head; thick, strong legs; and a long tail. The male is larger than the female and often has a thick, magnificent mane on the head, neck, and shoulders. Lions tire easily and spend up to 20 hours a day resting. Although male lions rule the pride (a group of lions numbering up to 15 individuals), lionesses do most of the hunting. Along with their formidable agility and speed—they are capable of short bursts of up to 40 miles per hour—lions use group cooperation and clever strategy to make a kill. Often, several members of the pride will act as "beaters," chasing their prey—usually zebra—into an ambush area where other lions are hidden. A lion can bring down a full-grown zebra with a single swipe of its powerful forepaw.

An adult male can gorge up to 90 pounds of meat during a single meal.

Injury

For treatment of wounds, see Bites, Gorings, Maulings, and Shock, p. 110.

A single lion killed 300 people in a Tanzanian town before being shot.

Throughout history, lions have been both feared and revered.

PECCARY

HOW IT GETS PEOPLE

Species: Tayassu angulatus and Tayassu pecari

HOW IT GETS PEOPLE

HABITAT

CLIMATIC ZONE

RATING

The American naturalist W. T. Hornaday wrote that "an enraged peccary, with his thirst for blood, is, to anyone not armed with a rifle or first-rate spear, a formidable antagonist." In Sonora, Mexico, one A. J. Requa learned just how formidable these brutish little creatures can be. Attacked by a large sounder, or herd, of peccaries, Requa took refuge in a nearby tree. But the peccaries did not give up, even when Requa began shooting at them from his perch. "They were chewing the tree and climbing over each other trying to get at me," he wrote. "Each shot laid one out, and each shot seemed to make them more and more furious, as

Peccary

they would rush at the tree and gnaw the bark and wood, while the white flakes of froth fell from their mouths." The enraged peccaries kept Requa treed for hours; he eventually had to tie himself to the tree to keep from falling out.

Name/Description

Peccaries are small, piglike, omnivorous ungulates (hoofed animals). The two primary species are the collared peccary (*Tayassu angulatus*), found in the southwestern United States and Mexico, and the white-lipped peccary (*Tayassu pecari*), found in Central and South America. The peccary is a rugged, noisy, ornery little critter with a stout body about 3 feet long and 18 to 22 inches high at the shoulder. A full-grown peccary can weigh up to 60 pounds. Peccaries have a long, rubbery snout for rooting out food, small eyes, pointed ears, and a conical head. Their hair is very coarse, and some have short manes. Peccaries are armed with a formidable pair of tusks about two inches in length. They are excellent swimmers, leapers, and runners and are known for their endurance.

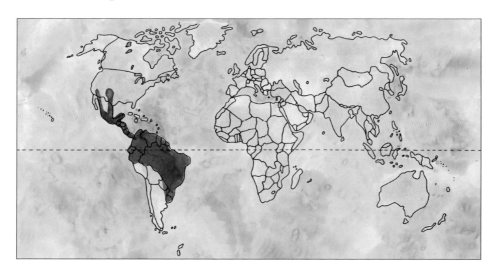

Dangerous Mammals

Peccaries travel in large sounders that can number as many as 200, and they usually range throughout an area of about 2 square miles. To mark their territory, peccaries rub the large musk gland on their back against rocks and bushes. While foraging, they snort and grunt constant-ly to keep in touch with one another. A sort of barking cough is used to warn others of danger. When they are annoyed, they make a threatening rattling noise by gnashing their teeth together. Peccaries are extremely protective of their young and will fight to the death to defend them. The entire sounder will often come to the aid of one of its members if it is attacked.

Injury

Peccaries usually attack en masse and thus inflict multiple wounds with their tusks. For treatment, see Bites, Gorings, Maulings, and Shock, p. 110.

Prevention

• If you are confronted by a single peccary or a sounder, climb a tree or a tall structure.

Peccary

The agile peccary can leap to a height of six feet
from a standing position.

Peccaries are noisy creatures; in addition to their
constant grunting, they may rattle, cough, or squeal.

PIT BULL TERRIER

HOW IT GETS PEOPLE

Genus: Canis

HOW IT GETS PEOPLE

HABITAT

HABITAT

CLIMATIC ZONE

RATING

The pit bull terrier—man's best friend, or man's worst enemy? Pit bull advocates praise this dog for its faithful and obedient character, its steady disposition, its intelligence, and even its love for human children. The dog's detractors—and it has many—revile the pit bull as a killer, a "land shark" that will attack without provocation, tearing flesh and crushing bones with its powerful jaws. Indeed, the pit bull has become the most controversial of domestic animals; after a spate of particularly

Pit Bull Terrier

savage maulings in England during the spring of 1991, Home Secretary Kenneth Baker sponsored unprecedented parliamentary legislation that would require the extermination of the entire pit bull population in Great Britain.

Name/Description

No one can deny that the pit bull terrier, known originally as the Staffordshire bull terrier, has had an exceptionally bloody history. The breed has its origins in 19th–century England. British dog breeders, hoping to combine the attributes of the terrier with those of the bulldog, crossbred the two. The result was the bullterrier, a canine fighting machine. A compact powerhouse of a dog with a short, smooth coat of various colors, short legs and tail, and a broad head with viselike jaws, the pit bull excelled at the "pit sport" of ratting, in which the dogs would chase and kill large numbers of rats in a pit, and bear baiting, in which the dogs would be set upon a chained bear in a pit. Soon, pit bull owners began fighting the dogs against one another, even after dogfighting was

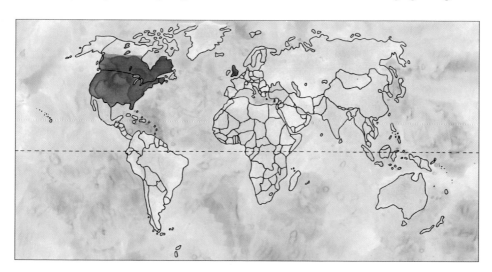

made illegal. Large sums of money were bet upon these dogfights, and owners began to breed and train their pit bulls specifically for the purpose of fighting other pit bulls. Thus, a race of warrior dogs was born.

Dogfighting was eventually stamped out in England, only to be re-born again in the United States. The resurgence began in the 1970s, mostly in rural areas of the South and West, where men gathered to watch fighting dogs battle to the death. Two magazines—the *Texas Pit Dog Report*, and *Pit Dogs*, published in Florida—kept dogfighting enthusiasts up-to-date on the latest breeding and training techniques. Once again, owners began to breed their dogs for the sole purpose of tearing other dogs to pieces while spectators wagered on the outcome.

Although it was illegal in almost every state, the unsavory sport of dogfighting spread, and by the 1980s clandestine matches were being held in numerous inner-city areas of the United States. Owning a dan-gerous pit bull became something of a countercultural status symbol in many cities, amateur "backyard" breeders began to sell pit bulls to people who wanted them as pets or guard dogs, and the number of pit bulls grew steadily. Many people soon found that they could not handle the ferocious animal and simply turned them loose, boosting the stray population. Those dogs that came from a combat bloodline inevitably began to manifest their breeding, and reports of people—and especially children—mauled and killed by pit bulls became commonplace.

Injury

The primary physical attributes of the pit bull are its powerful neck, chest, and jaws, which make it a tenacious and devastating biter. Once it sinks its teeth into something in anger, it simply will not let go. Victims frequently have their flesh chewed down to the bone, and the bones themselves can be broken or crushed. For treatment, see Bites, Gorings, Maulings, and Shock, p. 110.

Pit Bull Terrier

In the 1980s, pit bulls, which were used as pets and as guardians, attacked and killed many children.

Infection

Like all canines, pit bull terriers can carry rabies; for symptoms and treatment, see Rabies, p. 113.

POLAR BEAR

Species: Thalarctos maritimus

HOW IT GETS PEOPLE

HOW IT GETS PEOPLE

HABITAT

HABITAT

CLIMATIC ZONE

RATING

Although the grizzly bear has a frightful reputation as a hulking, super-powerful killer, many Arctic hunters believe firmly that the most formidable of the great bears is the polar bear. The polar bear is larger than the average grizzly and is certainly the most powerful of the ursine family. Furthermore, most grizzly bear attacks are the result of chance confrontations between humans and bears in the wilderness. The polar bear, on the other hand, is a cold-blooded killer; it is the only bear that will actually stalk—often for days at a time—and then kill human prey. The Inuit of the north believe that once a polar bear has chosen a certain person as prey, it will hunt that individual relentlessly.

Name/Description

The polar bear (*Thalarctos maritimus*), also known as the sea bear, water bear, Greenland bear, ice bear, and, by the Inuit, *nahnook*, is a huge, cream-colored carnivore widely distributed throughout the Arctic region. An adult male can grow to a height of 12 feet (when standing upright) and can weigh as much as 1,750 pounds. Compared to other bear species, polar bears have a long neck and a smallish, flat head. Zoologists consider the polar bear to be a marine mammal, for it is most at home in the water. A superb and tireless swimmer, the polar bear can cover great distances in the water; a thick layer of fat and air spaces within its coat give it a natural buoyancy as it propels itself with its wide, webbed forepaws. Polar bears have been sighted far out at sea, hundreds of miles from land, swimming along steadily with cubs in tow.

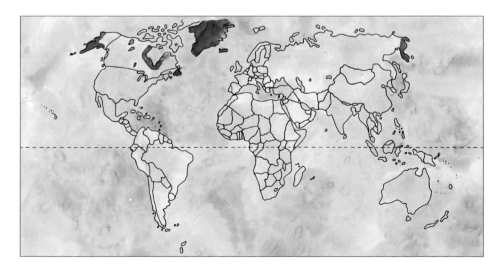

Polar bears also move well over the ice of the arctic regions; they have hair on the soles of their feet, which gives them traction on the ice, and they can run as fast as 35 miles per hour—swift enough to chase down a reindeer. The polar bear's keen eyesight—the best of any species of bear—allows it to detect movement a mile away, and a special third eyelid, known as a nictitating membrane, keeps the bear's eyes clean and moist and protects them from ice glare. The polar bear's usual prey is the seal, but it also feeds on sea birds, small land animals, reindeer, fish, vegetation, and berries. Polar bears are clever, patient hunters. When stalking a seal, they have been known to push a block of ice ahead of them to hide their telltale black nose, and they may wait for hours by a seal's air hole in the ice for the seal to appear.

Polar bears are generally solitary but will form large aggregations around a major food source. The bears have a brief mating period, after which the female will hibernate (males do not hibernate) and eventually give birth in her winter den to a litter of 1 to 4 cubs. Mothers with cubs avoid contact with males, which may try to eat the cubs. The average life span of the polar bear is 25 to 30 years.

Injury
For treatment of wounds, see Bites, Gorings, Maulings, and Shock, p. 110.

Prevention
• In polar bear territory, avoid wearing sealskin clothing, which smells heavily of seal oil and thus may attract polar bears.

Polar Bear

With a single swipe from its massive claw, the polar
bear can kill a seal weighing a quarter of a ton.

Polar bears can swim for hundreds of miles in open
seas and can run at speeds of up to 35 MPH.

PORCUPINE

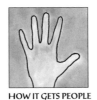

HOW IT GETS PEOPLE

Erethizon dorsatum

CLIMATIC ZONE

HABITAT

HABITAT

RATING

At first glance, the North American porcupine is a rather harmless, even pathetic–looking creature. It is a slow-moving, ungainly, unattractive little thing. But any other woodland creature or any human foolish enough to bother the porcupine will soon learn a painful lesson indeed, for this prickly little rodent is in no way defenseless. Cornered, the porcupine will stamp its feet, hiss, growl, and click its teeth. If this display fails to frighten off its antagonist, the porcupine will put its nose between its front feet and turn around, presenting its hindquarters and tail to the intruder. The porcupine's back and tail are covered with sharp, barbed quills—there are 240 quills per square inch. Usually the quills lie flat, but when the porcupine is threatened, the quills bristle. If the intruder continues to molest the spiny little mammal, the porcupine will lash out with its tail, driving dozens of the quills deep into its enemy's skin. At this point the invader—usually a fox, mountain lion, coyote, or dog—will withdraw, often with a snoutful of quills. (Contrary to popular legend, the porcupine cannot throw or shoot its quills at an enemy.) The quills have tiny, backward-pointing barbs that not only cause agonizing pain but also help the quills to work their way deeper and deeper into the victim's flesh, making them extremely difficult to extract.

Name/Description

Although the word *porcupine* comes from the Latin *porcospino*, meaning spiny, or prickly, pig. Porcupines are not pigs but large, heavily built rodents; their closest relatives are beavers and woodchucks. There are two subspecies of North American porcupine: *Erethizon dorsatum dorsatum*, a blackish porcupine found in the eastern United States and northern Canada, and *Erethizon dorsatum epixanthrum*, which is yellowish in color and found in the western United States and southwestern Canada. The North American porcupine averages 34 inches in length and 15 pounds in weight. Its thick, heavy coat is covered with hollow quills of two to four inches in length, and a single porcupine may have as many as

30,000 quills. Just beneath the tip of each quill is a band of about 1,000 tiny, backward–pointing barbs, which make the quills a cruel weapon. Older quills become loose in the socket and are easily detached.

The North American porcupine is primarily arboreal, living mostly in evergreen and aspen woods and migrating from the mountains to valleys in cold weather. It feeds on evergreen needles and bark, twigs, leaves, and other green vegetation, fruits, and occasionally agricultural crops. The porcupine's favorite delicacy is salt, and it will go to great lengths to obtain it, often gnawing objects that carry remnants of salt from human sweat, including canoe handles, ax handles, and saddles. They will go into houses to sample salty tabletops or floors, and they have even been known to chew on automobile tires that carry traces of salt strewn on winter roads to melt the snow!

Not surprisingly, porcupine matings are brief and infrequent, even though couples are careful to avoid one another's quills. (Females raise their barbed tails to keep them out of the way.) Female North American porcupines have a 209–day gestation period and usually give birth to a single offspring, although occasionally twins are born. Newborn porcupines have soft quills that harden after a few days. In the wild, North American porcupines have a life span of about 8 years; in captivity, they have been known to reach the age of 20.

Injury

Porcupine quills inflict deep, painful puncture wounds. Often, the barbed quills become imbedded in the skin and work their way inward and can cause infection and damage to internal organs.

Treatment

The quills should be removed immediately, the affected area should be cleaned thoroughly with an antiseptic, and the wound should be covered. Deeply imbedded and broken quills may require surgical removal.

Porcupine

Porcupines mate briefly, infrequently, and very, very carefully.

Prevention

- Be on the lookout in porcupine territory. If you encounter a porcupine, leave it alone.

- If you close up a cabin for the winter, leave a block of salt outside to protect it from invasion.

RAT

HOW IT GETS PEOPLE

Species: Rattus norvegicus and R. rattus

RATING

CLIMATIC ZONE

CLIMATIC ZONE

CLIMATIC ZONE

HABITAT

HABITAT

Not long ago in New York City, a young couple was awakened in the middle of the night by the screams of their 18-month-old son. To their horror, they found the infant bleeding from several bites on the ear, neck, and face. The guilty party—a large, bold New York City rat—was still in the room. The enraged father attacked the rat with a broom. The rat responded by sinking its teeth deep into the man's leg; it then turned and bit the mother. The family cat, which had been kept as protection against rodents, could not come to their aid—it had been killed by rats the week before. An estimated 1,000 people, mostly children, are annually bitten by rats in New York City alone, and it is now believed that there are as many rats in the world as there are people.

Rat

Name/Description

The mammalian order Rodentia (the largest of the mammalian orders) is made up of 1,000 species of rat. The most adaptive and, with the exception of humans, the most destructive mammals on earth, rats are truly ubiquitous, thriving in just about every kind of habitat the planet has to offer. But the two most common rats, the Norway rat (*Rattus norvegicus*) and the black rat (*Rattus rattus*), also known as the roof rat, are usually found in close proximity to humans, and in great numbers. The Norway rat, which is larger and more aggressive than the black rat, is usually 12 to 19 inches long, including a 6 to 8 inch tail, and weighs between 8 and 24 ounces. Its fur is grayish brown with paler underparts. The black rat is generally smaller, with darker fur. Both species have large, hairless ears and their long, scaly tail has but a few sparse hairs. They have a pointy snout, and like most rodents, they are equipped with a constantly growing set of incisors, which must continually be honed down to size. If they are not, these teeth can become tusklike, preventing the rat from shutting its mouth and chewing.

Rats need a lot of water and will even gnaw on pipes to get it.

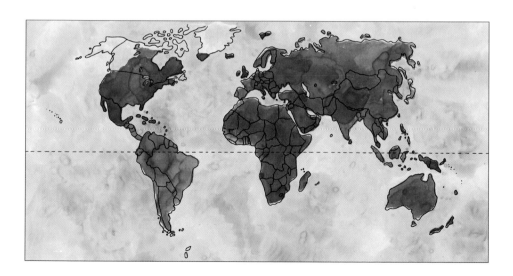

Dangerous Mammals

They will eat just about anything. Rats in the country will eat grain, seeds, nuts, and insects; they will also raid farms and chicken coops, and they have no fear of nibbling on larger animals. They especially like toenails, often biting humans on the toes, and they have even been known to gnaw on the feet of elephants. Their consumption of agricultural crops is devastating. Annually, rats eat or destroy enough of the world's grain to feed 130 million people. The superadaptable urban rat will eat toothpaste, glue, shoe leather, bars of soap, plastic, insulation, wiring, and power cables; they hone their incisors on the tougher materials, even gnawing on crumbling concrete. Rats are excellent climbers, swimmers, tunnelers, and leapers, and they can squeeze their flexible skeletons through the tiniest of openings. They are fierce fighters. Most cats, and even some dogs, are no match for a large, cornered Norway rat.

Norway rats and black rats live in colonies, or extended family groups. In the country, they inhabit burrows and underground lairs connected by networks of tunnels. In more urban areas, they live in ruined houses and buildings or in the walls, cellars, attics, crawl spaces, and foundations of structures still inhabited by humans; in dumps and sewers and subways; in parks and abandoned lots; in the bowels of stadiums and auditoriums; and generally in all the cracks and spaces and holes that riddle our cities. They are social mammals, and Norway rats tend to live in colonies that can have as many as 200 inhabitants. They often travel in large packs. Norway rats and black rats reproduce prolifically. A female is fertile at the age of three months and can breed year-round, mating just a few hours after giving birth and, after about a three-week gestation, producing litters of up to 12 offspring. Thankfully, rats have a relatively short life span of about a year.

Injury
Rats' teeth can inflict serious puncture wounds. For treatment, see Bites, Gorings, Maulings, and Shock, p. 110.

Rat

The resilient rat can survive radioactive fallout as well as a five-story fall without injury.

Infection

Rats carry numerous diseases that are harmful to humans. In the 14th century, rats were responsible for the spread of the bubonic plague, or Black Death, which decimated Europe. Today, rats transmit typhus, jaundice, amebiasis, tapeworms, trichinosis, tularemia, and rabies. For symptoms and treatment of rabies, see Rabies, p. 113.

Prevention

- Keeping down the booming rat population is difficult, especially in urban areas, where rats have no natural enemies. Various rat traps, poisons, and other extermination methods have proven only moderately effective in combating rats. It seems it is hard to fool a rat; rats have been known to sample poisoned bait and then to wait for a reaction before continuing the meal. Even if they can be tricked into taking the bait, immunity is quickly developed because they reproduce so rapidly, and a few generations later the rats will be unaffected by the poison. They also seem to learn how to spring traps without getting caught in them, after which they remove the bait and eat it in safety. The best way to keep your home rat-free is to keep it clean—where there is garbage, and especially food refuse, there are rats.

SHORT-TAILED SHREW

HOW IT GETS PEOPLE

Genus: Blarina

CLIMATIC ZONE

HABITAT

HABITAT

HABITAT

RATING

It is a ravening beast, feigning itself gentle and tame, but being touched it biteth deep and poisoneth deadly. It beareth a cruel mind desiring to hurt anything, neither is there any creature it loveth." This description of the short-tailed shrew comes from Edward Topsell's *History of Four-Footed Animals*, written in the early 17th century. Roger Caras, a more contemporary wildlife writer, has a similar opinion of the world's small-est—and hungriest—mammal: "If it were as big as a collie and kept the same rate of metabolism, it would be far and away the most dangerous animal alive, venom glands or no." Writer and naturalist Jack Scott described a painful close encounter with a shrew. Scott's retriever brought him a shrew and dumped it in his hand. "I thought the shrew was dead," Scott wrote, "but suddenly he came alive fiercely, biting. It was like the sting of a bee, the swelling was slight, but where I was bitten by the tiny jaws the area was inflamed and painful. The next morning I felt like I had had a three-day bout with bourbon, a sickly, dehydrated, hang-over feeling that lasted all day."

Name/Description

The short-tailed shrew of North America (four species of genus *Blarina*) is a tiny mammal resembling the mouse but more closely related to the mole. It grows to only three to four inches in length, including the tail, and weighs between one-fifth and four-fifths of an ounce. It has soft, brownish fur; a long, pointed snout; tiny ears and eyes; formidable teeth; and strong paws for grasping prey, digging, climbing, and building its nests. The short-tailed shrew is a solitary and territorial creature, living mostly beneath ground cover. It marks its hunting grounds with scent

and defends them fiercely against intruders. It makes a variety of high–pitched chirps, buzzes, twitters, and clicks, and is thought to use echolocation like bats and porpoises. (Echolocation is the use of sound waves to locate an object.)

The two most notable features of the short–tailed shrew are its voracious appetite and its venomous bite. The shrew has a metabolism that has been described as a "blast furnace"; its heart rate is 1,000 beats per minute. Primarily an insectivore (an animal that feeds on insects), it needs to eat every two hours to stoke this furnace and may starve to death within seven hours if it finds no food. Shrews can consume twice their own weight in food in a single day. The short–tailed shrew uses venomous saliva to subdue its prey—and to protect itself as well, which is extremely unusual in mammals. The venom is produced in glands in the lower jaw and flows forward along a groove between a pair of lower incisors.

Toxicology
The venom of the short–tailed shrew is neurotoxic (affecting the nerves) and proteolytic (able to break down protein material).

Symptoms
A short–tailed shrew bite causes localized pain, redness, and swelling in the affected area. Some victims experience a general malaise. Symptoms usually disappear within a few days.

Treatment
Clean the wound with antiseptic. An analgesic may be given to relieve the pain.

Short-tailed Shrew

Short-tailed shrews are high-strung, solitary creatures with "perfectly foul dispositions."

Prevention

• If you encounter a shrew, do not pick it up unless you are wearing heavy gloves.

SOLENODON

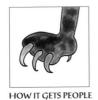

HOW IT GETS PEOPLE

Genus: Solenodon

HOW IT GETS PEOPLE

HABITAT

HABITAT

HABITAT

HABITAT

CLIMATIC ZONE

RATING

The solenodon is a mysterious shrewlike creature that only recently came to the attention of modern zoologists. Because of their decreasing numbers, limited geographic distribution—they are found only in Cuba's Bayama Mountains, in southwestern Haiti, and in the north-eastern Dominican Republic—and reclusive habits, researchers still have very little data on them. The native inhabitants of Cuba, Haiti, and the Dominican Republic, however, are more familiar with these odd mammals. They have reported that solenodons cannot walk in a straight line, and indeed, these animals ambulate in what is called an un–guligrade manner. Looking as if they are running on their toes, they waddle along quickly but erratically, often tripping over their own feet and tumbling head over heels. Solenodons are also known to have an unpredictable temperament; they frequently attack one another vicious–ly, and there are reports of them tearing apart chickens with their strong claws. Like their distant relative the short–tailed shrew, solenodons have venomous saliva, and when Haitian solenodons fight one another, even slight wounds can be fatal, for unlike most other poisonous animals they are not immune to their own venom.

Name/Description

There are only two species of solenodon: the Cuban solenodon (*Solenodon cubanus*), also known as the *alamiqui*, and the Haitian solenodon (*S. paradoxus*). They are primitive; fossil evidence shows that solenodons were in existence 30 million years ago. Solenodons are odd–looking animals. They have a stout, ratlike body of up to one foot in length, and

their legs, claws, and head are disproportionately large. They have a long, scaly tail and a bristly snout that is almost long enough to be called a trunk. Their ears are small and partly naked, and their eyes are tiny. The Cuban solenodon's head and neck are yellowish, but the rest of its body is darker; its fur is heavier on the lower parts of its body and thins out toward the top. The Haitian solenodon is smaller and differs in coloring, with yellowish underparts and muzzle and a brownish black body. The solenodon's forefeet are especially large, with five strong toes equipped with prominent, slightly hooked claws.

By night, solenodons hunt insects (the Cuban solenodon is the largest of the insectivores), worms, mollusks, small vertebrates, and occasionally fowl. By day, they find shelter in caves or in hollow logs, or they may dig themselves an underground burrow. Solenodons make various noises. In moments of excitement they grunt like pigs or let out birdlike cries and shrieks. They also emit high-frequency clicks for possible echolocation (the use of sound waves to locate an object). Solenodons have a venom apparatus that is much like the poisonous shrew's, and their claws and teeth are also formidable weapons. Nevertheless, when they are threatened by a superior opponent—such as a dog, a cat, a mongoose, or a human—they will often simply freeze and hide their head, a practice that has helped to bring the Cuban species to the brink of extinction.

Injury
The solenodon's sharp teeth and claws can penetrate and tear the skin, and venom will pass into the wound via the animal's saliva.

Toxicology
Solenodon venom is believed to be neurotoxic.

Solenodon

Although the solenodon wasn't officially discovered until 1833, fossils suggest that they lived in North America more than 30 million years ago.

Symptoms

A solenodon bite will produce immediate, localized pain and redness. Shooting pains and general discomfort may follow.

Treatment

Clean the wound with an antiseptic. Administer an analgesic for pain. There is usually a full recovery after a few days. See also Bites, Gorings, Maulings, and Shock, p. 110.

Prevention

• Do not pick up or play with solenodons.

TIGER

HOW IT GETS PEOPLE

Species: Felis tigris

HOW IT GETS PEOPLE

CLIMATIC ZONE

CLIMATIC ZONE

CLIMATIC ZONE

HABITAT

HABITAT

RATING

If you could use one word to desribe the tiger, it would be awesome," writes Jack Scott in his book *Speaking Wildly*. "Anyone who has sat in a tree in the Indian jungles at night as I have, watching this magnificent animal walking along a cartroad in the white moonlight, knows what I mean. So beautiful and perfectly proportioned that he seems cast in gold–bronze, the tiger is a living sculptural masterpiece. . . . He is so suddenly gigantic there beneath you that he doesn't seem real; so lordly and graceful as he glides in a movement that I liken to moonlight itself."

Tiger

Words such as *awesome, lordly, graceful,* and *beautiful* are frequently used to describe the tiger. *Terrible* is another, for a man-eating tiger is a beast of almost mythical proportions. One legendary man-eater killed at least 500 people in the jungle-covered hills of eastern India between 1959 and 1965. Entire villages were abandoned during this tiger's reign of terror. The *Hindustan Times* reported that from 1978 to 1983, 110 people were killed by tigers in the Kheri district alone. And in the mangrove jungles of India's Sunderbans National Park, 659 people were killed during a 15-year period; many of them were fishermen who were pulled from their boats. In the swampy Sunderbans, as one observer noted, the native inhabitants "have been a standard part of the tigers' diet for generations."

Name/Description

The tiger (*Felis tigris*) is the largest and most powerful of the big cats. The magnificent Siberian tiger (an endangered subspecies) has been known to grow to more than 10 feet in length and to weigh as much as 600

pounds. Tigers are most numerous in India, but tigers in dwindling numbers can still be found in Manchuria, Korea, China, eastern Siberia, Indochina, Sumatra, Java, and Bali.

The tiger has a massive, well-formed head and a strikingly handsome face. Its coat has a base color of orange, red, or yellow with black stripes. A solitary, nocturnal cat, the tiger is a jungle or forest dweller that usually preys on deer, antelope, and wild buffalo. It hunts primarily by sight rather than by smell and usually ambushes its victims from close range. It has a tremendous appetite and can devour up to 50 pounds of meat during a single meal. Tigers can live for up to 25 years in the wild.

Injury

The tiger's sharp teeth and claws and its powerful jaws can inflict devastating injuries. When attacking humans, tigers often go for the head and then crush the skull. For treatment, see Bites, Gorings, Maulings, and Shock, p. 110.

Prevention

- In the Sunderbans in West Bengal, which may have the highest concentration of man-eating tigers in the world, various attempts at curbing the local tigers' appetite for human flesh have been made. Because some experts believed that the salty marsh water of the area made the tigers more ferocious, freshwater drinking ponds were dug for the tigers. Local villagers were given fiberglass throat shields, and electrified dummies that were dressed in human clothes and that gave off a human scent were set up in the forests. When tigers attacked the dummies, they received a 230-volt jolt.

- There is a new antitiger experiment under way in the Ganges River delta where tigers kill about 60 mangrove forest workers a year. Students at

Tiger

According to medical reports, one tiger attack victim's "neck had been broken; the right side of his face was crushed and the eye scooped out. His left kneecap had been removed, as if by a surgeon."

the Science Club of Calcutta, noticing that tigers usually attack humans from behind, fashioned masks with human facial features for the workers to wear on the back of their head. From 1986, when the project started, until 1989, no one wearing a mask had been killed, while 29 workers without masks were killed in an 18–month period.

VAMPIRE BAT

HOW IT GETS PEOPLE

Genera: Desmodus, Diaemus, and Diphylla

RATING

HABITAT

HABITAT

CLIMATIC ZONE

CLIMATIC ZONE

Few animals inspire the feelings of revulsion and loathing that the vampire bat inspires. A blood-drinking creature of the night, vampire bats have scalpel-sharp incisors that are perfect for shaving away the epidermis (the outer layer of skin) of their sleeping victims. The vampire bat is such a precise surgeon that its victim—usually a warm-blooded creature, such as a cow—feels nothing. When the underlying capillaries are exposed, the bat will feed, lapping up the flowing blood much as a

Vampire Bat

cat laps milk from a bowl. An anticoagulant in the bat's saliva keeps the blood from clotting, and thus the thirsty bat can drink for as long as a half hour. Often it is so gorged after such a meal that it can barely fly. And because of the anticoagulant in the bat's saliva, the wound will continue bleeding for hours; thus, human victims frequently awaken to find themselves covered in blood—a hair-raising experience. However, the actual amount of blood lost in such cases is moderate; the real danger presented by the vampire bat is rabies.

Name/Description

Bats are the only mammals capable of true flight. The range of the vampire bat (genera *Desmodus*, *Diaemus*, and *Diphylla*), begins in central Mexico and extends southward through Central America and into Argentina. Vampire bats are tiny, usually growing no larger than three and a half inches long, with a four-inch wingspan, and their bodies are covered with brownish black fur. Nesting in upside-down clusters inside caves, hollow trees, old wells and mine shafts, and abandoned struc-

tures, the vampire bat is most active during the hours before midnight. Cattle are its usual victims, but birds and other warm–blooded mammals are also attacked. It has good eyesight (contrary to popular sayings about the "blindness" of bats), a good sense of smell, and it also utilizes echolocation. It can move with quickness and agility on the ground as well as in the air. Female vampire bats can only give birth to one offspring per year, but the vampire bat has a life expectancy of up to 10 years in the wild.

Injury
The wound from a vampire bite is relatively insignificant in itself, but there is the possibility of infection.

Infection
The primary danger associated with the bite of the vampire bat is the possibility of contracting rabies. For symptoms and treatment of rabies, see Rabies, p. 113.

Treatment
The wound should be thoroughly cleaned immediately. Secondary infections may be treated with antibiotics, and an antitetanus shot may be necessary.

Prevention
• In vampire bat territory, be sure that tent openings are well netted and windows well screened.

Vampire Bat

The vampire bat may consume so much blood in a single meal that it is unable to fly.

The vampire bat's bite is almost painless and rarely wakes a sleeping victim.

WOLF

HOW IT GETS PEOPLE

Species: Canis lupus

HABITAT

CLIMATIC ZONE

CLIMATIC ZONE

RATING

Wolves, perhaps more than any other mammal, have a bad reputation. But is the medieval conception of the wolf as a nocturnal marauder, a devourer of helpless grannies and little girls, justified? Over the years, tall tales and folklore have clouded the issue; thus, according to Jack Scott, "the wolf, actually among the most interesting and noblest of animals, emerged as wildlife's worst villain."

The wolf first acquired its reputation as an evil creature during Europe's Thirty Years' War (1618–48), a seemingly endless, bloody affair that left the countryside littered with hundreds of thousands of corpses, year after year. At dusk, packs of wolves would emerge to feed on the abundant dead. Although the wolves were simply taking advantage of an available food source, this behavior was viewed with horror by villagers. Other aspects of the wolves' appearance and behavior—their striking eyes, their eerie howling, their uncanny intelligence, their ability to "disappear" into the twilight—added to the aura of supernatural malevolence that surrounded them. When the war ended, men turned to slaughtering wolves instead of each other. Ever since, the wolf has been relentlessly exterminated in all of its natural habitats, if not as a threat to humans then as a threat to livestock, and today it has vanished completely from many areas where it once thrived.

Only recently, through the work of dedicated naturalists and zoologists, has a clearer, less hysterical picture of the wolf begun to emerge. Grisly stories of wolf attacks on humans still surface here and there—in 1962, in Turkey, villagers armed with axes and scythes supposedly battled a pack of man-eating wolves for seven hours—but these accounts are questionable at best. In North America, which has the largest continental population of wolves, there are no documented cases of nonrabid wolves attacking humans. Instead of a ravenous, cunning

man-eater, the wolf is now being seen for what it is—a remarkable and even admirable creature of the wild.

Name/Description

The wolf (*Canis lupus*) is the largest member of the canid family, which includes the coyote, the fox, the jackal, and the domestic dog. Wolves were at one time found throughout the Northern Hemisphere; today, there are still viable populations in the Soviet Union, China, parts of eastern Europe, Canada, and Alaska. Remnant populations hang on in parts of western Europe, Mexico, and Minnesota. Wolves vary in size from habitat to habitat, weighing from 45 to 175 pounds, measuring from 5 to 6 1/2 feet in length (including the tail), and standing from 26 to 36 inches tall at the shoulder. (The largest of the wolves is the North American timberwolf.) Wolves have a broad chest, small pointed ears, and long legs. Their doglike faces are handsome and well formed, with arresting eyes and extremely powerful jaws. The fur of the majority of wolves is of a smoky grayish color, but various other shades and color combinations are common, and there are also pure black and pure white wolves.

Wolves are carnivorous, and they prey primarily on large hoofed mammals, such as caribou, elk, deer, and moose. They are peerless hunters, usually stalking in cooperative packs and killing the young, aged, or sick members of a herd. Wolves have superb eyesight, hearing, and sense of smell, as well as a remarkable capacity for endurance; they can run as fast as 25 miles per hour and have been known to run without stopping for hours through deep snow. They are perhaps the most social of all the mammals. A wolf pack, which can number anywhere from 5 to 36 wolves, is a highly cohesive unit with a strict, well-ordered hierarchy. The pack is ruled over by a dominant male and his mate (known as the alpha male and alpha female), who are mated for life. Often, the alpha male and female will be the only members of the pack to mate; this "birth control" prevents a pack from overpopu-

Despite their violent reputation, loyal wolves mate for life, take care of the old, adopt orphans, and live in large, peaceful communities.

lating their territory and thus overburdening their food resources. A wolf pack's territory ranges from 50 to 5,000 square miles; it is marked by scent and jealously guarded from other packs. (Many experts also believe that wolves demarcate their territory by howling.) In the wild, a wolf's life span is usually about 10 years.

Infection

For symptoms and treatment of rabies, see Rabies, p. 113.

APPENDIX I:
Bites, Gorings, Maulings, and Shock

One does not have to be lost in the African bush or wandering through the rain forests of South America to be bitten, gored, or mauled by an animal. In the United States, 1 million people per year require hospital treatment because of animal attacks. The primary culprits in these incidents are dogs (man's so-called best friend), but bears, cats, rats, bats, hamsters, coyotes, bulls, raccoons, possums, ferrets, wild pigs, goats, horses, and moose—not to mention nonmammals such as snakes and alligators—are responsible for their share of injuries as well.

The nature of an animal attack will depend upon the animal itself. Many mammals, such as dogs, coyotes, rats, and bats, will use their teeth to bite their victim, which will usually result in lacerations and puncture wounds. If the animal has extremely powerful jaws, like the spotted hyena or pit bull terrier, crushed, fractured, and broken bones may result as well. Other mammals may use their claws to scratch, tear, and maul; the most notorious mauler is the grizzly bear, but a stray cat can inflict a painful mauling as well. And many of the larger hoofed mammals, such as moose, rhinos, elephants, and bulls, use antlers or horns to gore and will also trample a victim. (Elephants have even been known to crush people by kneeling, stepping, or sitting on them.) Deep puncture wounds, crushed and broken bones, and severe internal injuries may result. And the danger does not end when the attack does, for there is a serious risk of infection caused by microorganisms that may be present in the animal's saliva or on its claws, paws, horns, or tusks. Virtually all injuries sustained from an animal attack require tetanus prophylactic (protection from disease) measures, and the threat of rabies must also be considered (see Rabies, p. 113.) In the event of a serious animal attack, immediate first aid may prove to be the difference between life and death.

For gaping abdominal wounds or profuse bleeding from an extremity:
• Cover the wound with a clean cloth, gauze, or sheet dressing.

• Apply direct pressure to stop the bleeding.

• In the event of a severed artery, apply a tourniquet—a band made from a belt, tie, or another similar object—above the wound to slow the bleeding.

• Keep the victim prone, warm, and calm.

For a puncture wound in the chest:
• Cover the wound with a clean dressing.

• Wrap and knot a rope, belt, tie, or scarf around the chest to keep the wound closed.

• Keep the victim prone, warm, and calm.

For a puncture wound caused by the bite of a dog or a smaller animal:
• Clean the wound immediately and thoroughly, using antiseptics if they are available.

• Apply a clean dressing.

• Press firmly on the dressing to control bleeding.

Shock

In addition to the injuries that may result from a serious animal attack, the victim may also go into *shock*. Shock is a condition characterized by the failure of the circulatory system to maintain an adequate blood supply to vital organs. Symptoms of shock include hypotension (abnormally low blood pressure); oliguria (diminished urine output); hyperventilation; cold, clammy, and cyanotic (bluish) skin; a week and rapid pulse; drowsiness; mental confusion; and anxiety. If left untreated, shock can be fatal.

For initial treatment of shock:
- Use blankets or available clothing to keep the victim warm.

- Keep the victim prone, with the legs slightly elevated to improve circulation.

- Be sure the victim is breathing freely, and be prepared to provide respiratory assistance if necessary. Keep the victim's head turned to one side in case of vomiting.

APPENDIX II:
Rabies

It is said to be one of the most agonizing ways to die. The Greeks called it *lyssa*, or madness, and thought it only affected dogs. The Romans gave us the modern name—rabies—which comes from the Latin *rabere*, to rage, and in France it is still known as *la rage*. The disease manifests itself in a particularly appalling manner, often driving its victims into a frenzied madness before it finally kills them. Usually associated with dogs, rabies can be acquired by any mammal—including humans.

Pathology

Rabies, also known as hydrophobia (fear of water) because of the disturbed reaction to water it induces in victims in the latter stages of the sickness, is an acute infectious disease of the central nervous system, caused by a rhabdovirus that can be carried (usually in the saliva) and transmitted by almost any mammal. In the majority of cases, infection occurs when the victim is bitten by an infected animal and virus-containing saliva enters the wound. Rabies can also be contracted through exposure of mucous membranes or skin abrasions to infected saliva. There have been rare cases of respiratory infection as well, caused by the inhalation of moist air in a cave infested with rabid bats, and a small number of recipients of transplanted corneas have contracted the disease because the donors were infected but did not realize it.

Dangerous Mammals

When the bullet-shaped rabies virus enters the body, it penetrates the nerves and then migrates to the spinal cord, and then to the brain, where it multiplies. As the virus spreads, it causes a severe inflammation of the brain and spinal cord, a condition known as encephalomyelitis. From the brain, the virus travels outward through efferent nerves, eventually reaching the salivary glands.

Symptoms

The onset of rabies symptoms may occur a few days after the virus is contracted, or they may not develop for as long as a year. The usual incubation period, however, is 30 to 50 days. The symptoms progress through four stages. At first there will be irritation, itching, and pain at the site of the wound. This will be followed by restlessness, anxiety, headache, fever, loss of appetite, lethargy, nausea, and a sore throat. During the second stage there will be periods of violent, uncontrollable rage alternating with periods of sudden, listless calm. This is also when hydrophobia appears; despite a profound thirst, the victim's attempt to drink water may result in violent contractions of the throat. The lower jaw may drop, there will be difficulty in breathing, and the characteristic foaming at the mouth will begin. In the third stage the victim becomes uncoordinated and moves as if drunk, and there may be motor paralysis. In the fourth and final stage—which, mercifully, comes usually within three to five days of the first appearance of symptoms—the victim will die, usually from asphyxia, exhaustion, or general paralysis.

Treatment

Down through the ages, various rabies treatments have been tried, including submerging the wounded area in salt water for long periods or packing the wound with gunpowder and setting it on fire. The first successful rabies vaccine was developed by Louis Pasteur in 1884. Although it was said to be extremely painful—the treatment involved a series of 23 injections into the abdomen—and although serious side effects sometimes occurred, Pasteur's vaccine was used for almost a century. In 1980 a new vaccine was developed. In addition to being more effective, this vaccine requires only six injections in the arm and produces few side effects.

Prevention

- Any wound inflicted by an animal—whether you suspect it to be rabid or not—should be cleansed immediately and thoroughly with medicinal soap. See a doctor as soon as possible; the success of treatment decreases dramatically with delay, although the vaccine may still be worthwhile weeks or even months after infection.

- Be on the alert for strange behavior in nondomestic animals. Bats abroad during the day, for example, or wary animals, such as raccoons or foxes, showing little or no fear of humans, may indicate the presence of rabies.

- Spelunkers (cave explorers) should be vaccinated.

FURTHER READING

Ayensu, Edward, ed. *Jungles*. London: Jonathan Cape, 1980.

Caras, Roger. *Dangerous to Man*. South Hackensack, NJ: Stoeger, 1975.

Fossey, Dian. *Gorillas in the Mist*. Boston: Houghton Mifflin, 1983.

Freedman, Russell. *Animal Superstars*. Englewood Cliffs, NJ: Prentice-Hall, 1981.

Hayes, Harold. *The Dark Romance of Dian Fossey*. New York: Simon & Schuster, 1990.

Hopf, Alice. *Misunderstood Animals*. New York: McGraw-Hill, 1973.

Lopez, Barry. *Of Wolves and Men*. New York: Macmillan, 1978.

May, John, and Michael Marten. *The Book of Beasts*. New York: Viking Press, 1982.

Simon, Seymour. *Questions and Answers About Dangerous Animals*. New York: Macmillan, 1985.

Tee-Van, Helen Damrosch. *Small Mammals and Where You Find Them*. New York: Knopf, 1966.

Wendt, Herbert. *Out of Noah's Ark*. Boston: Houghton Mifflin, 1959.

INDEX

Dangerous Mammals

Index

Missy Allen is a writer and photographer whose work has appeared in *Time, Geo, Vogue, Paris-Match, Elle,* and many European publications. Allen holds a master's degree in education from Boston University. Before her marriage to Michel Peissel, she worked for the Harvard School of Public Health and was director of admissions at Harvard's Graduate School of Arts and Sciences.

Michel Peissel is an anthropologist, explorer, inventor, and author. He has studied at the Harvard School of Business, Oxford University, and the Sorbonne. Called "the last true adventurer of the 20th century," Peissel discovered 14 Mayan sites in the eastern Yucatán at the age of 21 and was the youngest member ever elected to the New York Explorers Club. He is also one of the world's foremost experts on the Himalayas, where he has led 14 major expeditions. Peissel has written 14 books, which have been published in 83 editions in 15 countries.

When not found in their fisherman's house in Cadaqués, Spain, with their two young children, Peissel and Allen can be found trekking across the Himalayas or traveling in Central America.

ACKNOWLEDGMENTS
The authors would like to thank Lisa Bateman for her editorial assistance; Brian Rankin for his careful typing; and Linnie Greason, Heather Moulton, and Luis Abiega for so kindly allowing their lives to be infiltrated by these creepy crawlies and ferocious fauna.

CREDITS
All the original watercolor illustrations are by Michel Peissel. The geo-graphic distribution maps are by Diana Blume.